Praise for *Wisdom for Life*

"Providing an easy-to-use framework for decision-making, Perry Atwal's *Wisdom for Life* is a modern and useful guide that allows us to optimize the choices we make as we proceed within our own life journey."

—GARY SAXTON, FORMER US ARMY INFANTRY OFFICER, BUSINESS EXECUTIVE, AND AUTHOR OF *100 MARATHONS AFTER 50: A RUNNER'S JOURNEY OF DISCOVERY, PERFORMANCE, AND GROWTH*

"Perry Atwal's book is perfect for gaining insight into life's complexities. What better way to become wiser than by learning from others? As world travelers and appreciators of world cultures, both Perry and I have acquired knowledge from all walks of life to share with others on their life's journey. *Wisdom for Life* is your pocket of gold to get you through life's challenges with ease."

—ORIT RAMLER, EXECUTIVE COACH AND AUTHOR OF *THE BOX OF LIFE: A GUIDE TO LIVING WITH PURPOSE AND PRESERVING WHAT MATTERS MOST*

"*Wisdom for Life* delivers clear, time-tested principles made practical. The standout benefit is usable clarity, turning complex choices into simple next steps. Atwal blends classic insight with real stories and concise exercises to help you make decisions about love, work, money, health, and faith. It's thoughtful, grounded, and immediately useful, page after page."

—SELINE SHENOY, AUTHOR OF *THE NOMADIC SOUL* AND HOST OF *THE DREAM CATCHER PODCAST*

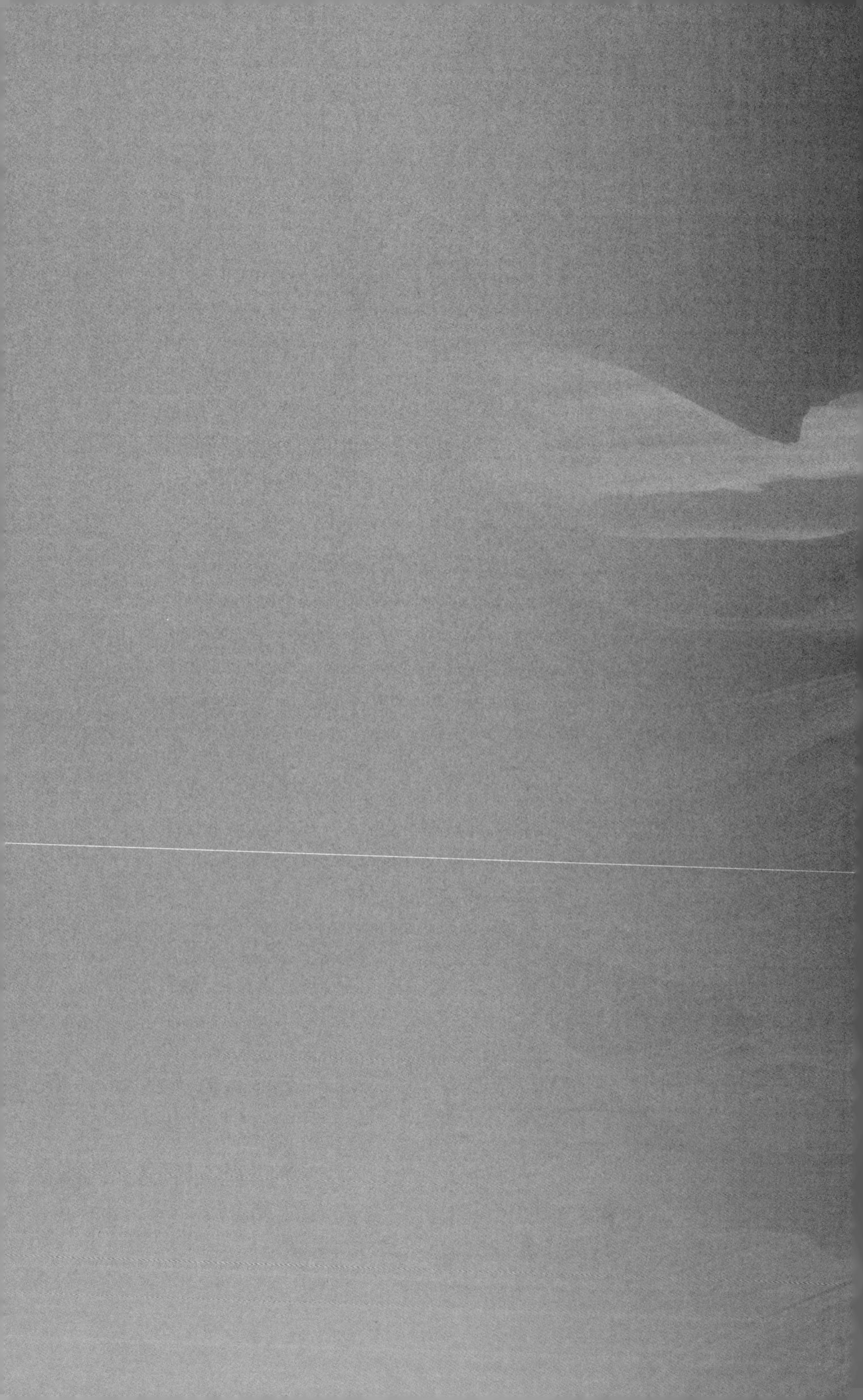

PERRY ATWAL

WISDOM *FOR* LIFE

TIMELESS INSIGHTS FOR *Cultivating Joy* AND *Growing Your World*

amplify
an imprint of Amplify Publishing Group

www.amplifypublishinggroup.com

Wisdom for Life: Timeless Insights for Cultivating Joy and Growing Your World

For more information, please contact:
Amplify Publishing, an imprint of Amplify Publishing Group
620 Herndon Parkway, Suite 220
Herndon, VA 20170
info@amplifypublishing.com

Library of Congress Control Number: 2025921364

CPSIA Code: PRV0226A

ISBN-13: 979-8-89138-861-1

Printed in the United States

This book is dedicated to my two greatest teachers: my wonderful children, Simrena and Shaan. I am eternally grateful for all of the wisdom that parenting you has provided!

Contents

"This book is intended to share the pieces of wisdom that have struck a chord in my heart over time."

—PERRY ATWAL

Acknowledgements

"Alone we can do so little; together we can do so much."

—HELEN KELLER

Writing this book has been an incredible journey, and what you read would simply not be possible without the valuable assistance of several important individuals.

Thank you to everyone who I have crossed paths with and who has colored my life to provide the material and inspiration for this book. I want to especially thank all of the folks at Amplify Publishing for turning my dream into reality.

And lastly, I would like to thank my incredible family. My energetic, adorable, and fun-loving kids have been my very best teachers, and my patient, caring, and ever-cheerful wife has been my rock on which all has been built. You are the best.

Introduction

"We cannot change the cards we are dealt, just how we play the hand."

—RANDY PAUSCH, *THE LAST LECTURE*

GENESIS

Knowledge and information keep on increasing at exponential rates. It is impossible for anyone to even come close to keeping up. However, I believe wisdom is in short supply. **The same principles that worked two thousand years ago are still evident today**. Everything has changed around us—people have changed, the environment has changed, our situations have changed. But wisdom keeps going strong. The way I see it, there are clear commonalities that can be observed across generations, places, and time, and understanding and applying these patterns equate to practicing wisdom. In effect, we are **learning from the past to make a brighter future**.

I remember a cold and rainy day in February, boarding my flight in Seattle. After driving for three hours and then waiting in lines to check in, go through security, board, and even go to the restroom, I was tired and a little irritable. I was not particularly looking forward to the five-hour flight to Washington, DC. For a moment, I reflected on how much I used to love flying as a kid, and how that love had evolved to how I felt now: namely, fatigued and really just wanting to be at my destination now.

Walking down the plane aisle, I saw the usual mixture of folks getting ready for the flight. Some were getting laptops out ready to work; others were getting blankets out ready to sleep. Where possible, I always liked to have a window seat. Not so much for the view but for the convenience of not having to get up for others. I put away my hand luggage, sat down in my treasured window seat, and then watched everyone else get on with some trepidation. Silently, I hoped that the family with the two screaming young kids would not be seated close by. The seating area around the boarding gate had not looked full, and given my above average height, I hoped the seat next to me would be empty so that I could stretch out a little.

No luck! An older gentleman made his way down the aisle, slowly squeezed his bag next to mine in the overhead bin, and collapsed into the seat right next to me. My initial feeling was one of frustration: *Oh well, here we go for five hours of mild discomfort.* But boy, was I wrong. This gentleman was about to change the course of my life forever.

We started off with some pleasantries, and he was easy to talk to. My normal rule when flying is to not engage in conversation with the person next to me until the last hour of any flight. That way, if they turn out to be annoying, they only bother me for a short amount of time. And usually, when meeting strangers, I am careful about saying too much quickly, as I never know who they are, what their angle is, or whether I should share information and engage in a deep conversation. But this guy was different. Despite our generational gap and many differences in our backgrounds, he seemed to know exactly what to say to make me feel at ease and to open up to him. It was only later that I figured out how. Not only did he have an immense amount of knowledge, but he also had advice on virtually every topic that we covered. School, work, flying, sports, love, money—he seemed to know it all. The combination of knowledge and advice had me nodding along, and it was the resonance of what he was saying with my own thoughts and beliefs that made our conversation feel enlightening.

The flight was over in no time, and for once, I actually wished it was longer! I didn't feel weary as I normally did after a flight. Instead, I felt as if something special had just happened. My fellow traveler left the plane with a slow shuffle, and as we waved goodbye, I felt immense gratitude towards the randomness of sitting next to such an incredible individual.

My cousin picked me up from the airport, and we went for a lovely meal. The food was divine. I felt relief at finally being at my destination, and it was wonderful to catch up, given we hadn't seen each other in a long time.

Just before dessert came out, my cousin asked, "So, Perry, what is it?"

"What is what?" I replied with surprise.

"What's happened to you? It's obvious that you sound different; you seem to have a lot more energy with a sparkle in your eye. What's changed?"

This was coming from someone who knew me very well, and so I took the observations seriously. Initially, I thought about my health, my work, my family, etc., and tried to figure out what was different from the last time we met. But then it dawned upon me. It was the incredible five-hour conversation that I had just had on the airplane! Without me even knowing, I had sprinkled some of my newfound wisdom into my conversation with my cousin, and it resonated deeply with him too!

"You seem more relaxed, and yet more energetic," he continued. I realized the wisdom shared with me on the airplane had achieved these contradictory feats. My mind was buzzing with new thoughts and wanted to do something with them—perhaps share with a larger audience—and that was both inspiring and energy-giving. On the other hand, the wisdom had provided some clarity and comfort with all the topics that we talked about. A deeper sense of "It's OK, these ideas are universal and ultimately helpful, so do not worry about what might happen" made me feel calm and content.

I shared with my cousin my experience on the flight and then went on to try and share as many of the nuggets of wisdom I could that had come my way just hours earlier. It was a very long night! When retiring to bed, I began to write some things down so that I could recall them when I got back to Canada. It dawned upon me that I would inevitably forget some of the wise words, as this is what usually happens in life. You hear some fantastic advice that resonates with you deeply, and it may stick with you for a while. However, then you forget, and the advice is only rekindled when you hear it again many years later.

While writing these random pieces of wisdom, the genesis of this book was formed in my mind. The original intention was to prevent forgetting the great pieces of advice I came across. I vowed to take notes every time a really wonderful quote or piece of counsel came my way so that it would remain fresh and useful in my life.

Once I had about thirty pages of notes, I realized there were many nuggets of wisdom that could be helpful for the people closest to me. Despite having no children at the time, I vowed to keep making notes and eventually pass this book on to my grandkids, with the accompanying words, "This is what Grandpa learned in his life."

Then, I got to sixty pages, and I started to organize the notes into the chapters you see in this book. At this stage, I thought to myself the material that I had accumulated could be useful to not just those close to me, but to anyone who wanted to learn more about wisdom. I incorporated my own commentary and observations from experiences I went through, and I began to share the book via summary presentations to my students.

Momentum gathered, and now we have the book you see before you. I never imagined that we would get to this stage, and I certainly did not start with the intention of publishing a book. But here we are. My vision for this book is quite simple:

To help people live happier lives through understanding and applying wisdom.

WHY ME?

You may be wondering why you should listen to (or read) my words instead of those of other infinite sources of information out there. Good question. From my research, **I don't believe there is any other book out there that houses the unique collection of wisdom that you see before you**. The breadth of topics and the level of detail for each topic are significant and go well beyond the usual books we see on wisdom.

Sure, there are many books on wisdom that are just full of quotes. While powerful, these quote-laden books do not include the same level of personal commentary and experiences that you will read in these pages. **It is this distinctive mixture of time-honoured wisdom housed with modern examples and real-life experiences that make this book special.**

I do not pretend to be *the* authority on the topic of wisdom, and I believe that no one really is. However, my unique and diverse background provides a solid foundation (or *competitive advantage* in business-speak) to impart the wisdom within these pages. I've worked in multiple cities across three continents (London, New York, Hong Kong, Shanghai, Madrid, and Vancouver) and with numerous clients across five distinct industries (aviation, chemicals, information technology, investment banking, and higher education). I've taught over twenty thousand students across multiple degree levels and topics, winning several teaching awards along the way, and I'm a parent to two children, one in her mid-teens.

In my life, I have seen some very clear patterns, patterns that are ubiquitous around the world in every industry and every geography, and that is what has made it into this book.

WHY WISDOM?

> *"Things do not change; we change."*
>
> —**HENRY DAVID THOREAU**

So, what exactly is wisdom? The *Oxford English Dictionary* tells us that wisdom is the "capacity of judging rightly in matters relating to life and conduct." But what does it mean to be right? Somehow, despite the lack of clarity in its definition, we seem to know wisdom when we see it. Wise people distinguish themselves from others in several ways:

- They stay **calm in a crisis** and can step back and see the bigger picture instead of getting stuck in the details.
- They are **thoughtful** and **introspective** and are often turned to when others seek guidance.
- They remain **humble** and recognize the limits of their own knowledge and ability.
- They can **adapt** and use their wisdom to apply to different, evolving situations.
- They can **tolerate uncertainty** and have a strong conviction towards what is right.
- They can **judge what is right or wrong** and are often proved correct in the long run.
- They are typically **optimistic** about life because they are **content** that everything happens for a reason.

Would you like to embody these traits? I believe most people would, and so the question becomes, "How can you become wiser?" We need to distinguish wisdom from intelligence. **You can be very intelligent** (**that is, know a lot**) **without being wise** (**that is, being able to exercise good judgement**). High intelligence does not guarantee better relationships or decisions, but high levels of wisdom, I believe, does. History is littered with incredibly intelligent people making ridiculously foolish decisions. **Becoming wiser will help you reach your full potential, find happiness, and find success**.

There seems to be a strong correlation between age and how wise someone becomes. Note, I'm not saying all older people are wiser than their younger counterparts, but simply that we all tend to get wiser as we age. Of course, our pace of change and starting points can be wildly different. Why does age help? I believe it is because we go through experiences that we learn from and observations that feed our judgement to improve over time. We also typically become less headstrong and stubborn.

STRUCTURE

This book of wisdom has been structured to provide maximum benefit to you, no matter what you are seeking. I want this book to be **practical**, and my fundamental goal is to **help** people, but I need your cooperation. For those who like to read a book from cover to cover, the chapters will take you on a journey covering all of the key elements of one's life to evolve a deeper understanding of wisdom, and to live wiser lives. Every chapter covers a major topic and has been carefully selected to ensure one has what they need to be wise. My intention is that rather than simply reading the material, you are engaged and active to make the most of our time together.

I do not want you to read the book, find the teachings in this book a little useful, and then forget about it. I want the book to help you make **permanent and positive changes to your quality of life**. To this end, at the end of every chapter, you will find summaries and key learning points as an overview of what was covered and a reminder of what to take away. Exercises are then provided to deepen your understanding and to raise your personal awareness, that is, how the material relates to your unique life. Finally, there are **reflection questions** that are intended for you to ponder in your own time and at your own pace to internalize and incorporate the learnings into your daily life. You will get the most out of the book if you complete the exercises and take a little time to reflect on the questions listed at the end of every chapter.

Gaining wisdom is a highly personal journey, and the reflection questions are usually short and vastly open-ended to allow the tailoring of thinking to your own inimitable situations. Again, I want to help you as much as possible and, from my nearly twenty years of teaching, can confirm these summaries, exercises, and reflection questions are some of the best ways to really make the most of your newfound wisdom.

Note, you might feel uncomfortable when answering the reflection questions, and that is OK. In fact, this discomfort symbolizes that you are growing. Consider how you grow as a person. Your current zone of comfort can be seen as a sphere around you, within which you are calm and content. You will then try new, unfamiliar things outside of your sphere. Once you have tried them a few times and gotten used to them, the exterior things are pulled into your sphere to make it bigger, and in effect, you have become a bigger person. This is how we all grow.

GROWING YOUR SPHERE OF INFLUENCE

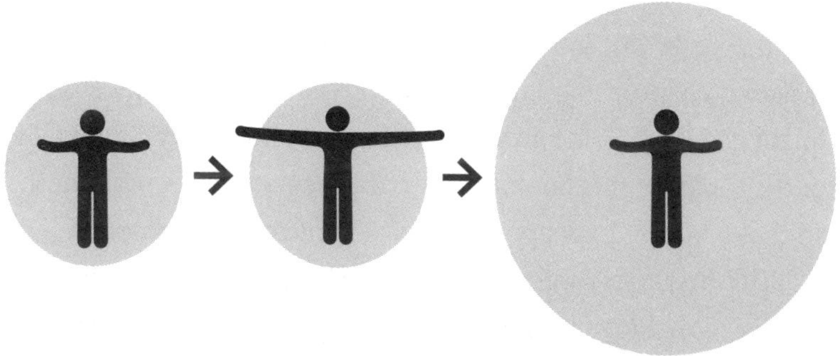

The different chapters of the book can be summarized in the following diagram:

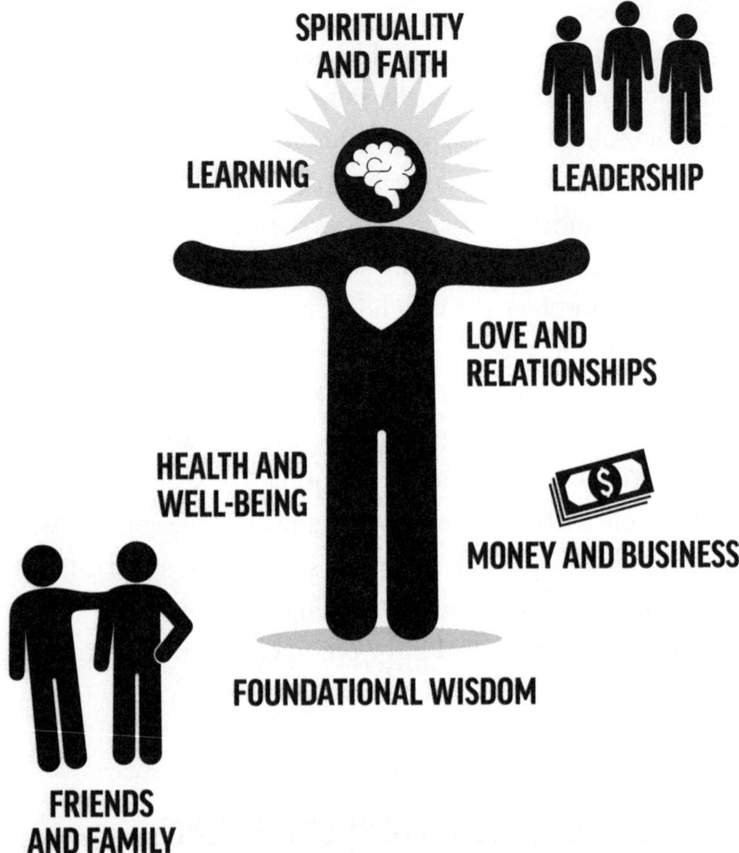

Before delving into the specific topics, we have a Foundational Wisdom chapter that lays the groundwork for all of the subsequent chapters. Some areas of wisdom traverse many (if not all) of the topics in this book, and it makes sense to start with these so that you can draw upon these skills for the later chapters.

The first two topics (Love and Relationships; Friends and Family) concentrate on all of the key people that you have in your life. Healthy relationships are good for you. **Supportive and loving relationships are more likely to make you feel happy, content, alive, and optimistic**. They also support you through challenging times and make the whole journey of life less stressful. Unfortunately, healthy relationships do not happen on their own. They need care, attention, and an understanding of our differences and what binds us together.

Our third topic, Health and Well-Being, delves directly into ways to make you feel physically stronger, fitter, and bursting with life. **Your aim is not just to survive but rather to thrive in this world**. It is very difficult to be your best if your body does not support you, and this chapter provides many pieces of wisdom to optimize your well-being.

In our capitalistic world, you have to be comfortable with money. It is not just about earning lots (although that certainly helps) but creating a mindset that embraces money and grants you financial freedom. You do not want to have to worry about money. The amount of worry we typically endure related to money (paying bills, where we can live, what to do in the future, and so on) is significant and unnecessary, and this chapter will help you overcome the most common pitfalls related to finances.

What exercise is to the body, learning is to the mind, and we need to look after our extraordinary mind. Our chapter on Learning discusses methods to expand your mind (by, for example, travelling), and how to ensure you stay sharp and educated to meet the challenges of the future. Technology keeps on advancing at frightening rates, but nothing has come close to matching what we can do with our minds, and so we have to look after them. We have no idea what will happen in the future, but if we have a clear, sophisticated, and wise mind, we will be able to deal with anything that comes our way.

There are some questions that are very difficult or, indeed, impossible to answer. Who are you? Why are you here? Who or what is God? What happens when we die? We cannot answer all of these questions definitively, but our penultimate chapter on Spirituality and Faith is intended to make you feel more comfortable with your place on this earth and more secure knowing that it all happens for a reason.

Finally, we will look at Leadership. Once you have developed yourself, the next target is to develop others and to use your skills to create great advances in the world around you. No matter how incredible you are, there is only so much that you can do alone. The ultimate test of a Leader is to gain more followers, and in this final chapter, we will discuss how to increase your influence and compound the difference that you make in this world.

All of the topics are linked, and improving in any one will have a positive effect on all of the others. For example, if you can get your body into an optimal shape where you feel an abundance of energy most of the time, you will have better relationships, you will learn more, you will be more content, and you will be there to lead others to further heights. If you have solid, supporting, and loving relationships at home and with the closest people to you, then you have extremely strong pillars that will allow you to get stronger (both mentally and physically), and embark on creative business adventures to increase your income.

For those of you who would like to focus on one part of your life, or who are looking for advice in some areas more than others, the chapters are independent and can be read in any order (outside of this Introduction and the next chapter, Foundational Wisdom). I believe all of the chapters are important, and it is extremely difficult to become wiser overall while neglecting any of the key areas. However, you may choose to jump right to what you are most interested in or need most help with. You can also return to this book at any time in the future and get immediate value by going directly to your interest, without worrying about the need of building up chapter by chapter.

Every chapter has a wealth of information, personal stories, quotes from others, and other relevant material that is intended to strike you at different levels. Like any dense collection of ideas, you will likely find new gems to help you every time you read or reread any chapter. Some of the writing has been deliberately layered so that, depending on your circumstances and level of awareness, you will find assorted pieces that will help you.

I understand that you may be anywhere along the spectrum of wisdom, but be assured that we are in this together. There have been times in my life when I have struggled and felt lost with what is really going on. I have felt that life was happening to me rather than that I was actually living. This book summarizes all of the crucial pieces of information that have helped me get to where I am today, and I know it will help you significantly too.

Everyone, from a relatively immature youth to a wise old person, can find value in this book. We are going places, you and I, and I invite you to learn, to grow, and to use your wisdom to make both your life and all of our lives better. Ultimately, that is what this book is about—becoming happier and making more of a difference. One of my favorite stories on happiness comes from John Lennon:

"When I was five years old, my mother always told me that happiness was the key to life. When I went to school, they asked me what I wanted to be when I grew up. I wrote down 'happy.'

They told me I didn't understand the assignment, and I told them they didn't understand life."

—JOHN LENNON

Are you ready? Let us begin.

CHAPTER 1

FOUNDATIONAL WISDOM

"A house must be built on solid foundations if it is to last. The same principle applies to man, otherwise he too will sink back into the soft ground and becomes swallowed up by the world of illusion."

—SAI BABA

We will begin our journey into wisdom by considering elements that are universal and that can be applied to all other sections of your life. Subsequent chapters are organized into broad topics that mirror different parts of your life, such as Love, Friends, Money, and so on. There are, however, a few pieces of wisdom that traverse all topics, and it makes sense to address these first with the goal of being able to draw from this chapter skills that will help you learn and implement advice in the rest of the book. We will categorize these elements into two areas: **the Importance of Perspective** and **the Mindset of Gratitude**.

THE IMPORTANCE OF PERSPECTIVE

"It's not what you look at that matters, it's what you see."
—HENRY DAVID THOREAU

Perspective is the way we view and interpret the world around us. We gain perspective through our life experiences, our values, our beliefs, and our current state of mind. **Perspectives are important because they shape how we behave in situations**.

As an example, my daughter used to play on a baseball team where one of the grandparents watching was extremely loud. During our first few games, I found the loudness (and quirkiness of one person chanting by themselves) off-putting, a little shocking, and even rude. After getting used to his shouting and realizing some methods behind the madness—it turned out the shouting was highly motivating to the team and also added to the atmosphere of games—I actually started to enjoy the experiences.

My perspective had shifted. My initial perspective of the shouter being rude may well have caused me to react angrily or in an upset manner when the shouting started. However, after a while, I actually began to enjoy it and felt lucky that we had such a vocal supporter. The situation was the same, and the shouting was the same, but my perspective had shifted so that instead of potentially having an awkward situation to ask him to be quieter, I actually felt more like giving him a hug to show appreciation for his efforts!

By learning to alter our perspective, we can gain new insights and find creative solutions to life's challenges. To develop a complex understanding of an issue or idea, you need to be able to look at it in many different ways. The answer is not always right in front of you but, sometimes, on the periphery. Your expanding perspectives will allow you to become more creative because you have more information to draw upon and, therefore, more places to potentially make links and breakthroughs.

Perspective is dynamic. As your surroundings, situations, experiences, colleagues, etc. change, your perspective may change too. When you are hungry, for example, you notice all the food in close proximity. When you are full, the food around you does not seem as attractive. This is the reason why you should never go grocery shopping when very hungry—you are likely to get too much because your stomach is growling!

UNDERSTANDING OTHERS

No two people will see a situation or issue in exactly the same way. Your perspective matters, of course, but it's largely limited by your own experiences and background. To become wiser, we need to be able to understand situations from different perspectives. We need to consider other people's beliefs, experiences, and viewpoints. Wise people are always asking good questions because they understand that they do not know everything, and others around them have very different perspectives. **Wise people want to learn.**

Making the effort to understand different perspectives also builds empathy. Empathy nurtures trust. Through trust, you can build stronger relationships. Building and maintaining trust is a cornerstone of becoming wiser. It will allow you to:

- become a stronger leader to connect with and influence followers further;
- become a better friend and family member by being more open to others and having them be more open to you; and
- become someone whom others want to do business with.

Note, to really make use of perspective, you need to listen to other people's views. Be careful of only reaching out to people who share your perspective—they will reaffirm what you believe, but you may be missing something important that can only be revealed through diverse perspectives.

No matter how thin you slice it, there are always two sides, or multiple sides, to any situation, and you should keep this in mind when a problem arises in your relationships. How often have you heard about a situation from one person, and it seems like another person is being absolutely ridiculous? When you speak to the other person, though, they fill you in with some context and history that completely changes your view. Try to suspend judgement until you have found out as much as you can, for if you jump to conclusions and actions, you may just end up with egg on your face at a minimum, or far worse, a damaged relationship.

If you want to keep your relationships going, you will want to frame situations in ways that help you rather than hold you back. Be careful: Just as you can seriously love close people around you, you can also seriously hurt them. Only close people can hurt you—a stranger mouthing obscenities to you will do little long-term damage, but the same words from someone close could be devastating.

Remember to be fully present with whoever is in front of you. For example, it's not a good idea to praise your mother's cooking when you are eating something that your spouse just made for you.

Be really selective with the company that you keep. The people around you will have an inordinate influence on the quality of your life, how you feel, and how you approach the world. You have no choice in some areas (for example, with close family), but with others your choices towards where and whom you spend your time with will make all of the difference. A good rule of thumb is to try and surround yourself with people that lift you and inspire you to new heights. If you are the smartest person in your group of friends, then you will find it hard to get smarter. If you are the hardest worker in your group of friends, you will find it difficult to work harder. Spending time with those who are already achieving what you desire to achieve will help you get there quicker. But if things don't work out, don't burn bridges with anyone. You will be surprised how many times you have to cross the same river again in the future.

SHIFTING FOR GOOD

A quick example helps illustrate how perspective influences us. Imagine you are on a bus going down a busy street. You are with a friend—let's call him Henry—and you are both gazing out of the window.

When looking outside, you notice some birds flying around, and you are in awe of how they have learned to fly and how they are free to go almost anywhere. You marvel at how the road has been built up over the years, and how we have evolved to incorporate complex housing, transportation, and sewer systems to live in relative luxury. You marvel at all of the shops you pass, considering how brave some of these small business owners must have been to venture into business for themselves, rather than working for others. The sun is shining, and you are surrounded by so much positivity and potential—life is good!

Henry, on the other hand, sees a very different picture. The graffiti on some walls reminds him of the local gangs who have been infiltrating the neighborhood. Henry spots a homeless person and wonders why there are any homeless people when there is so much wealth close by. He sees some old buildings decaying and considers how the town has gone downhill from what it used to be like. Henry notices people who seem to be rushing around and not caring about those around them.

Now, both you and Henry are in exactly the same situation—riding a bus along a busy street, gazing out of the window. But you will both feel completely different because your *interpretation* of the world around you is completely different. You will get off the bus in a better mood and will be more likely to help others, and your enthusiasm may prove infectious. Henry, on the other hand, is likely to be more closed and pessimistic, and less likely to help anyone, because of his negativity. Whom do you want to feel more like?

Do you like to see the glass half empty or half full? Do people describe you as optimistic or pessimistic? Is your go-to reaction when experiencing something new to marvel at what's incredible, or to find the flaws?

My advice is to **think positive, especially when you don't know all the details.** Did that colleague roll their eyes, or might they have had something in their eye? If you don't know for sure, why not frame the situation in a light that helps you? If you think they rolled their eyes, you may start thinking negatively (*they don't care*). But if you pass it off as them possibly having something in their eye, then you don't feel the negativity.

Note, it's not about being blind or naïve to what is happening around you. I'm simply suggesting to take the positive road when you are not sure. Often, it's the **lack of information** or understanding that leads us to perceive situations in negative or unhelpful lights. Shift your perspective! Don't look at a request from your boss as a problem to address, but rather, an opportunity to shine. Don't look at a challenge as something that is going to be difficult and time-consuming, but rather, as an opportunity to grow and become better.

I saw a great example of how perspective affects how you feel while playing in the garden with my son and an elderly uncle. We were playing (a very homemade version of) table tennis, and the ball often went to the ground and needed to be picked up. After a while, I got tired of stooping over, so my uncle took my spot. I felt bad for him because he was in his mideighties, and I thought it must be so difficult for him to keep stooping down and picking up the ball, but he carried on.

Ten minutes later, I noticed that my son and uncle were still playing. When they finally stopped and my uncle sat down, I thanked him for having the energy and patience to keep playing with my son.

"It must have been so difficult for you to keep stooping," I said. "Thanks for sacrificing to make my son happy."

"What are you talking about?" he replied loudly. "I love it when the ball drops to the ground because it gives me another opportunity to stretch down and stay healthy!"

I had assumed that the inevitable strain of stooping regularly would be undesirable, but my uncle's wonderful response shifted my perspective and allowed me to see the situation in a far more positive light. Think of anything that is affecting you negatively right now. Is there any silver lining to the cloud? Is the situation making you stronger, wiser, smarter, or less likely to fall for the same mistakes again? Whatever is happening is still happening, but what you choose to focus on, or in other words, your perspective, is largely going to determine your attitude and how you feel.

To summarize, developing your powers of perspective by empathizing, really listening to and making an effort to understand others, keeping an open mind, and appreciating that there are many ways to look at anything will help you become wiser. You will become more understanding, build trust with others, and be able to creatively tackle any challenge that life throws your way.

THE MINDSET OF GRATITUDE

> *"Let us rise up and be thankful, for if we didn't learn a lot today, at least we learned a little, and if we didn't learn a little, at least we didn't get sick, and if we got sick, at least we didn't die; so, let us all be thankful."*
>
> **—BUDDHA**

No matter what your current life looks like or how much (or little) you have made progress towards worthy goals, your life will benefit from developing a mindset of *gratitude*. Gratitude is the quality of being thankful for what you have. You can experience gratitude in the short term if something works out the way you wanted, but we are going to talk in this section about long-term gratitude, which is more of a positive character trait that you can have all the time. **Gratitude changes your perspective of the world, because it frames whatever little you may have into joy and abundance.**

Having a gratitude-rich mindset bestows several benefits. Firstly, it lifts your mood and makes you feel more positive towards life by minimizing negative thoughts. When you are feeling down, one of the best remedies is to go into detail as to what you are grateful for. Gratitude also recognizes that there are forces outside of your control working to help you in life. You can be grateful towards many others (God, other people, work, animals, etc.) and not just grateful for things that have worked in your favour.

Every major theme in this book can be enhanced upon with a sense of gratitude.

Gratitude helps build and maintain relationships by making you want to help others more. When you come into wealth, gratitude will help you stay grounded. When learning, an attitude of gratitude will drive you on, humble you, and make you realize there is so much more to learn. Gratitude is a cornerstone of many religious and spiritual practices. You will feel better and come across as a person to get to know when you exhibit gratitude. Gratitude tends to be reciprocated and spreads quickly, so as a Leader, you will be blessing your followers with this exceptionally positive trait.

The research highlights many advantages of having a healthy sense of gratitude, including many proven mental benefits. Studies show that gratitude can improve happiness, self-esteem, and resilience, and in some cases, even induce a natural euphoria! Gratitude can also lower stress, anxiety, and depression; boost the immune system; and provide benefits for individuals who are in recovery for substance abuse and for post-traumatic stress disorder.

When you live in a state of gratitude, it doesn't mean that everything is easier for you or that you will not feel the pain and pressure of your normal life. It just means that you will be able to frame the world in a more positive light, and can therefore focus on what is important instead of getting overwhelmed.

Given all of the advantages of gratitude, your aim should be to incorporate thanks into your daily practices. I like to thank God whenever something positive happens to me. Even if I worked very hard and it was my effort that caused the good thing to happen, I still thank God for giving me the energy and ability to achieve the great result. And if things don't go so well (and this is a severe test), I will still try to thank God for things not going even worse!

For example, if I receive outstanding evaluations for a course that I've taught, I know that the main factors were the time I spent preparing and understanding the audience and topic, as well as using skills that I have developed over a long time. However, I will silently thank God for giving me the opportunity, helping develop the skills that I used, and making sure luck went my way with nothing unexpectedly bad happening.

I will talk about my daily walks and affirmations in our chapter on Health and Well-Being, but for now it's worth noting that my last affirmation is always one of gratitude. It ends my affirmations with an incredibly positive feeling, and keeps me balanced by not only asking for more (which most of my affirmations do), but also being extremely grateful for everything that has come my way. Consciously try to be more grateful over the next few days, and just see if you feel better in any way. If you do, you have learned one of the wisest practices possible.

Exercise

PERSPECTIVE AND GRATITUDE

The way you feel at any given time usually depends on the perspective or way that you frame the situation in your mind. We can all benefit from gaining perspective that is constructive, helpful, and positive rather than negative, limiting, and destructive. Sometimes, we just need to understand how lucky we really are. The following exercise will help you put things into perspective and can be a go-to exercise whenever you are feeling lost, sad, lonely, or overwhelmed.

- Close your eyes and take deep breaths: in through your nose for ten seconds, and out through your mouth for ten seconds.
- When breathing in, try to visualize all the abundance around you, and focus on what you are able to do daily.
- When breathing out, try to visualize or imagine all the toxicity and negativity leaving your body.
- After one minute of deep breathing, consider the following questions (with eyes still closed), and stick with each question as long as you like (you may have to repeat the exercise several times to get through all of the questions):
    - Who are the people in your life that have meant the most to you? What have they done, specifically, to support you?
    - What opportunities have you seen in the past year for your life (could be related to

school, work, community, or anything else)?

- What was a very nice compliment you have received in the past year?
- What do you have that many people around the world would love to have, but don't?
- How are you lucky?
- Name one way that you have helped someone around you in the past year.
- What new habit have you developed in the past year that has been helpful?
- What is one unexpected thing that brought you joy recently?

CHAPTER 2

LOVE AND RELATIONSHIPS

"Love is that condition in which the happiness of another person is essential to your own."

—ROBERT A. HEINLEIN

Love. What does it mean to love? Why do people fall in love (note the *falling* part)? What do you love? Why is it important to love? In my experience, when you love something, you go **beyond what is expected**. If you love your work, you will happily do more than what is required. People ask you for one thing, and you will give them three things, because you love the topic and are willing to go over and above; it feels as though it requires no effort. When you love someone deeply, you put their interests before your own and feel fantastic since you believe your purpose is more than just about yourself.

When you are in a serious relationship, you free up a lot of time and energy—time and energy that you would otherwise spend dating, hoping, and guessing. People in serious relationships have plenty of opportunity to get more things done. Good relationships also ensure that you are not drained by emotional roller coasters.

How do you know when you are in a good relationship? Simply, **when you care more about the other person than you do about yourself**. Unfortunately, love can be blinding. Love is far more powerful than any drug or addiction because it transcends all of your emotions. We all know people who have fallen in love, and all of a sudden, they seem to be behaving strangely and irrationally. As Douglas Yates put it, people who are sensible about love are incapable of it. Love typically heightens our senses but lowers our perception of what is really happening around us.

There is nothing wrong with staying single—some of the happiest people I know have deliberately chosen a single path. The key word, however, is "deliberate." The vast majority of us dream of finding our perfect love and believe the right person will enhance our lives considerably. We will therefore firstly look at how to find our right love, and then how to stay in love, for the rest of this chapter.

Remember, **relationships are sent to test us**. Without the immense highs and lows you experience with and because of other people, you would not learn and complete yourself. As Seneca tells us: "No man can live happily who has regard to himself alone and transforms everything into a question of his own utility; you must live for your neighbor as if you would live for yourself." Just remember to love yourself first. And note, love is a far broader topic than just loving another person, but for the purposes of this book, we will stick to getting that right partner.

FINDING THE RIGHT PARTNER

> *"We come to love not by finding a perfect person, but by learning to see an imperfect person perfectly."*
>
> **—SAM KEEN**

Love is the most powerful of weapons. Love the right person, and they will elevate your life to unimaginable heights, support you to achieve your lofty goals, make you incredibly happy, and lead you to live a fulfilling life. Love the wrong person, and they will kill your dreams, destroy your relationships with others, and drag you down to the depths of (ironically) loneliness. **You need to choose whom you love wisely.** But how do you find that "right" person? Is it all down to luck? Is it about being in the right place at the right time? There are many things in life that you can control, and there are things that you cannot. The key is to focus on what is within your realm and to leave the rest to destiny. We will discuss more about this topic in chapter 7 on Spirituality and Faith.

For example, you may have a crush on someone who is seemingly out of reach. They are already in a happy relationship, and the last thing you want to do is rock the boat or put yourself and the other person in an awkward situation. Should you pursue them? Maybe it does make sense to let them know how you feel (although once you have crossed that line, there is usually no going back to being just friends). However, you need to understand that **you cannot change someone if they do not want to be changed**. You cannot *make* someone love you. All you can do is be someone who can be loved. The rest is up to them.

Maybe the timing is wrong. Maybe this person is not the right one for you. Maybe you should move on to find someone who is available at this time. Having this awareness and rational view of reality can help, because it will save you from pursuing the wrong person and experiencing lots of heartache and time lost. But as we have already said, love can be blinding and fool you into thinking someone is perfect for you when they really are not. I find getting the opinions of those you trust to be extremely helpful in this situation. Others will not feel the same emotional roller coaster that you may be experiencing when you fall for someone. Remember that, just like great achievements, **great love involves great risk**.

On the topic of emotions, it's worth examining how helpful or destructive they can be. Sure, emotions can amplify how you feel at any time, and when things are good, there is nothing that makes you feel more alive than powerful positive emotions. There is, however, a flip side to this ecstasy. Imagine the following: There is a person—let's call him Tom—that annoys you a great deal. Whenever you come across Tom, he says or does something that triggers a negative reaction in you. For example, Tom finds it amusing to mock your accent, given that you are from a different part of the country.

You are now about to go into a room where you know Tom is seated. You know exactly what Tom will do or say because Tom always does the same thing: an impression of your accent. But you think to yourself, *No, I am a smart person, and I will not be bothered by what Tom will inevitably do or say.* You walk in confidently and take a seat at the table.

Within five minutes, Tom is making fun of your accent, and you find yourself getting upset or angry just as you always do. What on earth happened? You knew what Tom was going to do—he does the same thing every time! Well, what happened is that you got *emotional*. As you walked in you were thinking logically, with your brain, about the likely teasing, and you mentally prepared for what was coming your way. But, to your chagrin, when Tom started doing his thing, you became emotional. Suddenly, the logical part of your brain shut down, and your emotions came straight from the heart.

The point is that our emotions can be destructive if we don't learn how to keep a handle on them. In fact, one of the pillars around the concept of *Emotional Intelligence* is recognizing and handling our emotions before they become a problem. Positive emotions can improve your mood and physical health, increase your optimism, and build stronger social connections. Negative emotions (although useful in some situations to provide motivation and information) typically take you in the opposite direction, making you weaker and more pessimistic and potentially damaging your relationships.

When searching for the right partner, it is imperative that **you like the way your prospective partner treats *other* people**. Yes, that's right: not so much how they treat you but others around you. Why? Well, it's almost a given that they will treat you well (they probably wouldn't get very far if they treated you poorly in the initial stages). Look for how they treat others. Do they bark at a server who gets the order slightly wrong? Do they let down friends at the last minute for no good reason? This is important because the way they treat other people is likely how they will treat *you* once the novelty and excitement of initially finding a partner wears off.

Let's talk about looks for a moment. You often hear the phrase "It's not about the looks; it's about the personality." In my experience, if someone utters this phrase, then rest assured that they are already with a good-looking partner! It is easy to give advice to others when you don't have to worry about it yourself. I'd like to go a little deeper here, so consider the following. When you first meet someone, I believe there has to be something raw about them that you find at least a tiny bit attractive. This could be the way they look, the way they walk, the way they talk, their humor, their smile, or anything that makes you think, *hmm*. If there is something raw, then this initial seed may grow until this person becomes the most attractive person in the world in your eyes. However, if there is absolutely nothing that stokes your fire at the raw level, that is, no seed of attraction, then it may prove difficult to evolve a relationship together. I'm not saying it's impossible, but I believe it is highly unlikely.

When you meet someone where there seems to be a mutual spark, how do you know if they will be right for you in the long term? We've all heard that opposites attract, and there is something about the variety of characteristics that can spice up a relationship. **Opposites may attract, but it is the *similarity in your beliefs* that keep you together.**

I believe it's not the values, per se, that are important to match with a potential partner, but rather the *order* in which you prioritize them. If you have a very similar hierarchy of values to another person, then you will typically see the world in the same way. You will interpret situations in a comparable manner and will come to similar conclusions in any situation. You will also likely make similar decisions, and it will be far easier to cohabit with this partner, since you will be on the same page most of the time. Couples who are wildly different may enjoy the ride for a while, but these relationships rarely last once the uniqueness loses its shine.

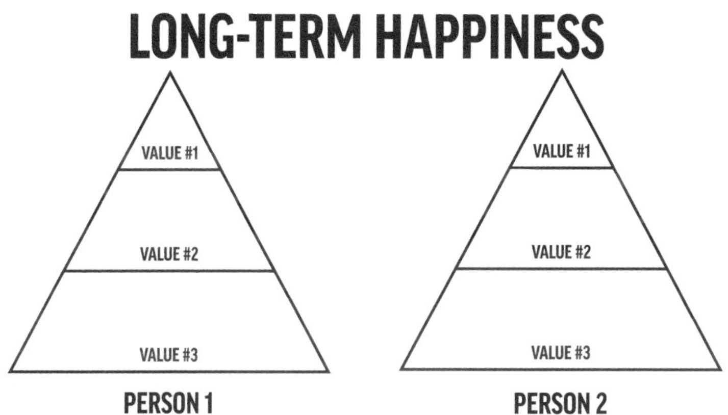

We all have personalities and nuances, and they come across over many dimensions. Let's take one dimension to illustrate the need for similar values. Let's call this dimension "planning." At one end of the spectrum, we have what we will call Planners, like my wife and me. These are people who constantly plan ahead how they will spend their time. For example, let's say we plan to meet another couple for a dinner next Friday. Not only will we as Planners commit this to our calendar, but we will also plan what we are going to do for the rest of that day. We will plan where to drop off the kids beforehand, who is going to drive, a visit to a store just before our dinner, what time we should leave work, and so on.

At the other end of this spectrum we have the Last-Minuters.

These are people who are inherently more spontaneous and will consistently change plans at the last minute. They often will not commit to events because they know they may not be able to follow through, will rarely use a calendar (or stick to it), and believe it's fine to "see what happens" or "go with the flow," rather than plan ahead. Now, neither end of the spectrum is right or wrong, but you can imagine how either extreme would drive the other to insanity.

For example, the Last-Minuters may say on Friday morning that they cannot make the dinner because something has come up. The Planners will clearly be highly annoyed, and not just because the dinner plans have fallen through, but also because the postponement will mess up all of the other plans they made (dropping and picking up kids, leaving work early, shopping at a store nearby, and so on). The Last-Minuters will not necessarily understand (or care) about how the Planners think, and they will justify their actions, because in their own world, they believe things change all the time and you shouldn't get upset over a small postponement. The closer you are to your partner on any such dimension, the more you will make the same decisions and interpret situations in the same way.

In strong relationships, folks are aligned on important, major dimensions, and this alignment helps pull people through the major differences in smaller, less important dimensions. In fact, I find that, over time, strong partners tend to move towards each other's positions on otherwise polarizing dimensions. Both sides tend to soften their stances and meet more in the middle, partly because they understand the bigger picture and partly to maintain harmony. This also helps explain why couples tend to become more alike over time—they have fewer polarizing interests. It also helps to mellow you out as you get older because you're not as stubborn in your beliefs and, therefore, not as affected if things don't go as planned.

I've also noted that finding your right partner becomes a little easier as you grow. As you get older, you need less time to assess if someone is right for you. When you are young (say under the age of twenty-five), you are still growing and changing a tremendous amount every year. If you are in a relationship, you can grow with the other person. However, once you get to, say, the late twenties, then you are pretty set in your ways and will not change too much over time. You have to love yourself to truly love another, and you will more likely have this confidence when you are a little older. Not only will you know yourself to a greater degree, but you will also have a better idea of what is important for you in another person.

You want to be with someone whom you love to talk to. As you get older, their conversational skills will be as important as any other. You also want someone whom you can share a silence with comfortably. As humans, we are typically not comfortable with silence and feel the need to break it when with others. When you can enjoy that silence together, you know you are relaxed enough to enjoy each other's company while not saying a word.

Try the following exercise with the next few people that you meet. Let them speak, and make sure they can see that you heard their words (by nodding, for example). But don't say anything. Let the silence linger. Most of the time, the other person will feel the need to break the silence. (Of course, let them know afterwards what you were testing. And point out that we do not typically embrace this type of silence.)

The rules are completely different in finding and developing relationships—they are not logical. In normal life, you can work very hard to get what you want. You are taught that hard work and discipline will make sure you realize your dreams. In relationships, it doesn't matter—working harder or doing more doesn't necessarily get you anywhere. I've lost count of the number of people I know who feel they have diligently done everything they possibly can to find the right person (dating apps, numerous introductions, etc.) and are still left frustrated and unable to acquire that special relationship. On the other end of the scale, there are many who do absolutely nothing and manage to secure their perfect partner by chance early on and, therefore, avoid all the heartache and roller coasters of dating and breaking up. Remember, there are things that you can control, and things that you cannot. Either way, knowing what you are looking for helps.

BEING THE RIGHT PARTNER

> *"I love being married. It's so great to find that one special person you want to annoy for the rest of your life."*
>
> **—RITA RUDNER**

Like most things, relationships can become stale. The key is figuring out how to make the relationship feel new by constantly renewing your interest in each other. The opposite of love is not hate, but rather indifference or boredom. It's worth looking at what happens to relationships over time. At the beginning, you typically paper over any cracks that may be apparent. You are so joyful to be in the relationship and caught up in the excitement and novelty of it all that the small issues just bounce off you. But after a while, those cracks become larger and larger and affect you in different ways.

For example, if your partner leaves the cap off the toothpaste, it may seem like a cute quirk when you are in the early stages of a relationship. But if it annoys you even a little, then rest assured it may turn into a major argument later on. It's not that the other person has changed (after all, they are doing what they always have done), but rather, it affects you more because you don't have the same tolerance being early in a relationship affords you. Watch out for the cracks early on, and try to fix them before they become a significant problem.

A long-term relationship is not just about *finding* the right partner but also *being* the right partner. When you are with someone, don't rely on that person for all of your happiness. Think of deriving all joy through being with each other as the same as facing each other. Instead, stand side by side and face life together. You might not always get love, but you can always choose to give love, and the more love you give, the more you will receive. If you love your mate and want the relationship to grow and evolve, you've got to learn how to close one eye and not let every little thing bother you. You and your mate have many different expectations, emotional needs, values, dreams, weaknesses, and strengths. You are two unique, individual children of God who have decided to share a life together.

Always be the first one to pay for something, whether it is a drink, a meal, or anything similar. Someone has to go first, and consider what it says to the other person. Not only does your kindness show them respect, but it can also tell you lots about the other person. If they feel the need to reciprocate (and this doesn't have to be by doing the exact thing you did for them), this may be a good indicator of how nice they will be to you in the future. If they don't reciprocate, then maybe they are distracted, overwhelmed, or simply not at the same level of kindness as you are. Yes, it may be easier for someone with wealth or a good job to cover this (compared to someone who is struggling to make ends meet), but in reality, the $10 to $20 you spend is not going to make much of a difference. (A $1,000 expense may be the difference between having heating or not next month, but a $20 deficit is highly unlikely to tip any scales.) By going first, you set the tone, and it also helps in creating a feeling of abundance (more on that later), which helps build your confidence and positive attitude—great attributes that will make you more attractive.

People are different, and we need to embrace our differences. It's also worth exploring how we change as we age. We typically grow in various directions and, in effect, are constantly becoming different people. You are different from the person you were one year ago, and very different from who you were five years ago. Your partner does the same. If you can imagine starting at a similar point, over time even small initial differences in direction result in huge differences later on.

Consider why we celebrate the longevity of relationships. We have a name and associated gifts and metals/gemstones for every major anniversary.

Figure 1

ANNIVERSARY GIFTS BY YEAR

YEAR	TRADITIONAL	MODERN	METAL/GEMSTONE
1ST ANNIVERSARY	PAPER	CLOCKS	GOLD
2ND ANNIVERSARY	COTTON	CHINA	GARNET
3RD ANNIVERSARY	LEATHER	CRYSTAL OR GLASS	PEARL
4TH ANNIVERSARY	FRUIT OR FLOWERS	APPLIANCES	BLUE TOPAZ
5TH ANNIVERSARY	WOOD	SILVERWARE	SAPPHIRE
6TH ANNIVERSARY	CANDY OR IRON	WOOD	AMETHYST
7TH ANNIVERSARY	COPPER OR WOOL	DESK SET	ONYX
8TH ANNIVERSARY	BRONZE	LINENS OR LACE	TOURMALINE
9TH ANNIVERSARY	POTTERY	LEATHER	LAPIS LAZULI
10TH ANNIVERSARY	TIN OR ALUMINUM	DIAMOND JEWELRY	DIAMOND
15TH ANNIVERSARY	CRYSTAL	WATCH	RUBY
20TH ANNIVERSARY	CHINA	PLATINUM	EMERALD
25TH ANNIVERSARY	SILVER	SILVER	SILVER
30TH ANNIVERSARY	PEARL	DIAMOND	PEARL
35TH ANNIVERSARY	CORAL	JADE	EMERALD
40TH ANNIVERSARY	RUBY	RUBY	RUBY
45TH ANNIVERSARY	SAPPHIRE	SAPPHIRE	SAPPHIRE
50TH ANNIVERSARY	GOLD	GOLD	GOLD
55TH ANNIVERSARY	EMERALD	EMERALD	EMERALD
60TH ANNIVERSARY	DIAMOND	DIAMOND	DIAMOND

Source: https://www.brides.com/gallery/wedding-anniversary-gifts-by-year-for-him-her-and-them

Why do we focus so much energy on marking these milestones? Think about what has changed in your life just in this past year. Consider how much you have learned, what you have been through, all of the ups and downs, the new people that you have met, the studying or work you have undertaken, the places that you have visited, and so on. These things all change you. Think of it as a minor five-degree change in the course of your life. Now, your partner has also gone through this five-degree change (give or take) within the last year. (Note: Seismic events in your life can cause a far higher degree of change, such as births, deaths, extremely difficult times, breakthroughs in your spiritual development, and so on.)

Given you both change about five degrees a year, it's a minor miracle that you find each other interesting after a number of years. So how do couples do it? Two points to ponder: First, and most obvious, they keep working on the relationship. Successful couples don't typically become complacent. They constantly look for new and exciting ways to cement and build their relationship, whether it's trying new things or showing affection and respect in different ways. They constantly renew their relationship and don't allow it to become outdated.

Second, given they like to spend so much time with each other, their five degrees of change significantly overlap. For example, they take up new hobbies together, go through ups and downs together, experience new vacations together. Therefore, the couple is not actually deviating a total of ten degrees from each other every year. They actually find even more in common overall every year, and the relationship flourishes rather than withers. To facilitate this closeness, it is much easier when they have some very deep values in common. Remember, values do not typically change year to year. Your values, which largely came from when you were younger and were heavily influenced by family, culture, neighborhoods, and teachers, remain the same. Again, the core values and the hierarchy of values are key.

Inevitably, you will have disagreements. Note, I use the word "disagreements" when I could easily use a word like "arguments," "fights," or "run-ins." Why is this important? Well, what do you think of when I say "argument"? Most people will picture a heated situation where both sides are getting emotional, possibly shouting at each other, or worse. It conjures up an image of a highly negative situation, whereas the word "disagreement" seems far more civilized. It implies that there is a difference of opinions and, more importantly, a problem to be solved together. There can be many solutions to a problem, and they can all be correct. Be very careful of the words that you use, as they influence your perceptions.

You cannot always agree with someone, but you can always come to an agreement. There is nothing wrong with saying, "Let's agree to disagree on this issue," and then focusing on how you can move on. This is very much how I believe the concept of consensus is misunderstood. Reaching consensus amongst a group of people does not mean that you keep going until everyone completely agrees. Rather, it is getting to a stage when everyone is committed to supporting the ultimate decision. Some may still not think it is the best way forward, but you agree to continue and back what has been decided.

Never go to sleep upset, and do whatever it takes to make sure that you have a peaceful mind when you close your eyes, including temporarily putting aside all differences. If you go to sleep with negativity dominating your thoughts, it will not only affect the quality of your sleep but also provide your subconscious a whole night of breeding further negative thoughts. In a relationship, it doesn't matter who is right or wrong. The important thing is for the relationship to be strong and for you both to be happy. Therefore, when in a disagreement, ask the question: Do you want to be right, or do you want to be happy?

Of course, things do not always work out well. If you come to the end of a relationship, try to disassociate feelings for that person from feelings of just being with anyone. It is lonely at first, but you likely don't miss *that* person so much as the intricacies of being with *any* person. You will have constant reminders of your relationship that will make you feel sad. But are you really missing that person, or do you just miss having someone to share a movie or dinner or time with? Love makes any inevitable loss worth it. There is a famous saying from Lord Alfred Tennyson: "'Tis better to have loved and lost than never to have loved at all." Just remind yourself often of this quote to ensure you make the most of the time you have together. In a relationship, the opposite of happiness is not sadness, but boredom.

On a lighter note, marriage is the best teacher of all. It teaches you loyalty, humbleness, patience, self-restraint, forgiveness, and a host of other qualities that you wouldn't have needed if you had stayed single! (Only kidding.) But life is just too short to marry the wrong person. And never marry someone whom you would not like to be divorced from! You must love deeply and passionately. You have to put everything into your relationship. You may get hurt, but it's the only way to live life fully.

SUMMARY AND KEY LEARNING POINTS

- Finding the right person to share a relationship with can be difficult and out of your control but, ultimately, incredibly rewarding and a pillar towards a happy and fulfilling life.
- You cannot change someone if they do not want to be changed. **You cannot make someone love you.** All you can do is be someone who can be loved.

- It is not just important to *find* the right partner, but also to *be* the right partner.
- Love is the most powerful emotion, but remember that emotions shut down the logical part of your brain. When making major decisions about love and relationships, make sure you have considered them from both emotional and logical frames of mind.
- You must like how your partner treats other people, for this is how they will eventually treat you.
- Opposites may attract, but it is the similarity in your beliefs that keep you together.
- The more similar your hierarchy of values is to your partner's, the better chance you have for a happy, long-term relationship, since you will interpret the world in the same way and make similar decisions.
- Finding a partner becomes easier as you age, because you understand both yourself and what you really want to a greater degree.
- Disagreements are inevitable, but how you deal with them (and how you frame them in your mind) will go a long way to maintaining a strong relationship over time.
- Be vigilant about what words you use to describe any situation or how you feel. Words are extremely powerful.
- Never go to sleep upset with your partner.
- If you come to the end of a relationship, try to dissociate feelings for that person from feelings of being with just anyone.

Exercises

VALUES

What are your most important values (sometimes called your core values)? Select ten from the following list of ninety-six of the most common core values. This may take a little time, so it may be easier to first scan the list and pick all the ones that mean a lot to you. Then, try to narrow those selected to the ten that resonate most:

Abundance
Acceptance
Accountability
Achievement
Adaptability
Adventure
Authenticity
Altruism
Balance
Beauty
Belonging
Boldness
Challenge
Citizenship
Community
Compassion
Confidence
Contribution
Cooperation
Creativity
Curiosity
Determination
Dignity
Diversity
Environment
Efficiency
Equality
Excellence
Fairness
Faith
Fame
Family
Financial Stability
Forgiveness
Freedom
Friendships
Fun
Generosity
Gratitude
Growth
Harmony
Happiness
Health
Honesty
Hope
Humor
Independence
Initiative
Innovation
Integrity
Job Security
Justice
Kindness
Knowledge
Leadership
Learning
Legacy
Love
Loyalty
Meaningful Work
Nature
Openness
Optimism
Order
Peace
Perseverance
Pleasure
Poise
Popularity
Power
Recognition
Reliability
Religion
Reputation
Resourcefulness
Respect
Responsibility
Risk-Taking
Safety
Security
Self-Discipline
Self-Respect
Service
Simplicity
Spirituality
Stability
Status
Success
Teamwork
Tradition
Travel
Trustworthiness
Truth
Uniqueness
Wealth
Wisdom

Once you have identified the ten, organize them into hierarchical order. How do you do this? Think of dilemmas—what would be most important for you? For example, let's say two of your values are integrity and success. Would you sacrifice your integrity, even only temporarily, to gain an advantage to achieve success? Would you consider taking steroids or other performance-enhancing drugs to become the best player in your league? If so, success would be a higher value then integrity.

Note, this exercise can be uncomfortable, but once you are clear on your hierarchy, then it will be easier to ascertain if a partner will be good for you long-term. You just need to figure out their values (through conversation and observation) and their hierarchy. If your hierarchies are similar, then you will see the world in similar ways and will make similar decisions.

STRONG RELATIONSHIPS

How do you know if you have a strong relationship? What should you be looking for when building a relationship? The checklist below is high-level and can help you determine the strength of your relationship. The more of these elements you can tick as being true, the stronger the relationship is.

- ☐ Regular, open, and honest communication.
- ☐ Mutual respect for what each other is trying or achieving.
- ☐ Regular intimacy.
- ☐ Shared sense of humor, where you can have a good laugh together.
- ☐ Shared household or menial tasks.

- ☐ Some getaway time without work, school, or children.
- ☐ Daily exchanges (e.g., a meal, shared activity, a hug, a call, a touch, a note).
- ☐ Common goals, interests, and views of your future life.
- ☐ Space for each of you to grow without feeling insecure.
- ☐ A feeling of safety with each other, where you're able to share your deepest hopes and fears.
- ☐ A sense of belonging together and assurances of commitment.
- ☐ Life feels more exciting with each other.
- ☐ You feel like you know each other really well.

Taking the last point above on knowing each other well, try the following exercise with your partner:

HOW WELL DO YOU KNOW EACH OTHER?

How well do you really know another person? You can use this test for a partner or anyone whom you consider to be close. Each of you should ask the questions of each other, and it may actually surprise you how much (or little) you know about each other, or how imbalanced the knowledge in the relationship seems to be.

- What is your favorite book?
- What are your three favorite movies?
- What is your favorite color? What is your least favorite color?
- Where is your favorite place to go on vacation?
- What is the one place in the world that you haven't been to and would really like to go?

- Which three values are most important to you?
- What is your go-to reaction to disagreements? Needing space, or wanting to talk it out immediately?
- What is the one place in the world that you have been to and will likely never want to go again?
- What is your favorite ice cream flavor?
- What are your top three favorite foods?
- What are your top three favorite drinks?
- What is your go-to karaoke song?
- What was/is your favorite subject at school?
- If you won a million dollars, how much of it would you give away?
- If you won $100 million, how much of it would you give away?
- Whom would you like to meet most in the world (who is still currently alive)?
- Which historical figure would you most like to meet (who is no longer with us)?
- If you could travel back in time, which year and where would you go first?

REFLECTION QUESTIONS

- What really matters to you in life? Do you need a special someone to help fulfill your goals?
- What matters most to you in a partner (regardless of whether you currently have one)? (Note: You may not want a partner, and in that case, this question is easy!)

- Have you behaved like the kind of person you would like to be with over the past week? How about the past year?
- If you have a partner, it is worth taking some time to evaluate how strong your relationship is and where you can improve. To get a good sense of its strength, consider the following questions:

    - Do you feel safe with your partner?
    - Can you tell them what you really feel in any situation?
    - Do you listen to each other's concerns without being judgemental?
    - Do you trust each other?
    - Can you be yourself around them?
    - Do you feel better in their company?
    - Do you inspire each other to achieve more?
    - Have you both changed for the better because of your relationship?
    - Do you regularly do things for each other without being asked and for no other reason than that they are your partner?
    - If you are in a relationship, how would others describe your relationship? (Think about friends, family members, and others around you.)

CHAPTER 3

FRIENDS AND FAMILY

"You don't choose your family. They are God's gifts to you, as you are to them."

—DESMOND TUTU

In our previous chapter we looked at love and how to find and be the right partner. But how about those you love whom you did not choose to bring into your lives: your family? And going a little further, how about those whom you choose to love, but not in an intimate or romantic way: your friends? These people, more than anyone else (except your partner if you have one), will influence you in every area of your life, and the way you treat them and think about them will affect how happy you become.

Needless to say, it is impossible to overstate the importance of managing these key relationships.

FAMILY TIES

> *"The bond that links your true family is not one of blood, but of respect and joy in each other's life."*
>
> **—RICHARD BACH**

Your immediate family usually dictates your home life, and **having a happy home life is critical if you want to reach your full potential.** If your home life is happy (and by happy, I mean there are lots of comfort, laughs, security, warmth, and love), then no matter what happens in your life in the outside world, you will be happy. Conversely, if you have a sad or miserable home life (typically lacking those wonderful feelings of comfort, security, and love), then even making a billion dollars outside won't matter. You will, overall, not be happy. Creating and maintaining a happy home life should be right near the top of all your priorities.

Family can become a problem. They typically know all of the buttons to press to make you upset, and they press them frequently. The *best* thing about family is that they are always *there for you.* You can rely on their loyalty and support no matter what, and that confidence provides an important pillar from which you can explore the world. The *worst* thing about family is that they are *always there.* You can't get rid of them, and occasionally they can make you feel frustrated or suffocated. Remember to never judge people because of their family. They didn't choose the family they belong to. Families can be thought of as a box of chocolates—mostly sweet, but there are always a few nuts included. You can, however, tell a lot about someone from the friends they keep. **Friends are the family that you choose,** and you can choose to continue or discontinue friendships.

If you have siblings, then you will share a bond like no other. Even if one or both of your parents were different, you will have likely grown up together in the same environment and will have therefore gone through many experiences together when you were highly impressionable and building the foundations for your life. As many people can attest, siblings can be completely different on a multitude of features. I have a very different personality than my brother, and I can cite numerous dimensions where my kids are at completely different ends of the spectrum. The bonds you share, though, are strong, and they will also determine how you build relationships in the future.

WHY KIDS MAKE SUCH A DIFFERENCE

> *"Insanity is hereditary. You get it from your children."*
>
> **—SAM LEVENSON**

When I look back at my life so far, I can easily split it into two distinct parts: before I had kids and after I had kids. I'm not saying that you have to have a child in order to feel fulfilled, but I do believe that there are certain emotions and roller coasters that you go through as a parent that I cannot imagine can be repeated with any other experience. The feeling of looking your kids in the eyes for the first time is special beyond words. Watching your kids move through various milestones (both obvious, such as birthdays, and less obvious, like when they can get in and out of a car by themselves) warms your heart like nothing else. Kids help complete you, because raising them tests all of your weaknesses. For example, if you are not usually patient, you will no doubt have to learn to become very patient over time.

If you have kids, they will change your life immeasurably. All of a sudden, you go from making decisions that will largely only affect your life to focusing almost entirely on these other small beings. All of your decisions, short-, medium-, and long-term, center around your kids. Short-term decisions such as "What are we going to eat tonight?" depend on your kids. Medium-term decisions such as "Where should we go on holiday?" depend on your kids and what they can tolerate. Long-term decisions such as "Which neighborhood should we live in?" depend on your kids. You go from thinking about yourself to thinking almost entirely about how your decisions will affect your kids. I believe this also explains why individuals experience midlife crises. For a number of years, as your kids are growing, virtually every decision you make has to consider the effects on your kids. Then, all of a sudden, they don't want to spend so much time with you, and you have a massive void in your life. Some people choose to fill the void with trying things they never imagined they'd try in their younger years, such as getting a motorbike or bungee jumping.

A hundred years from now, it will not matter how much money you accumulated, what kind of house you lived in, or the kind of car that you drove. But the world may be different because you were important in the life of a young person. The kids are literally our future, and we need to nurture them and teach them basic values so that they can survive without us. Indeed, this is a nice part of the job description for parents, and there are tremendous changes and phases that all parents go through. For example, it is ironic that during the first two years of a child's life, we are trying to get them to walk and talk, but for the next eighteen years, we are telling them to sit down and shut up. A great piece of advice I came across is that it is important to have a dog when your kids are teenagers. Why? Because at least someone will be happy to see you when you get home!

Having kids will dominate the life of anyone who chooses to do so. Unfortunately, the timing is usually in line with some of the busiest times that we have as employees and adults trying to figure out what to do with our lives. No wonder it can seem so overwhelming. There are several reasons why grandkids and grandparents get on so well. The grandparents were typically so busy when they looked after their own kids that they never really appreciated how much of a marvel it was to watch the kids grow. Now that the grandparents are older, they don't have to worry about the daily routine of looking after kids, so they can enjoy the moments with their grandkids for what they are: incredibly precious. They can give the kids back at the end of the day and not have to spend half the night dealing with a crying child. The other reason why grandparents and grandkids get on so well? Simple—they have a common enemy!

Like everything in life, there can be downsides to having kids. For example, sleep is a wonderful thing, and like most wonderful things, it can only be truly appreciated once it is not readily available—such as when you have children! Adults are always asking kids, "What do you want to be when you grow up?" As Paula Poundstone reminds us, this is largely because adults are looking for ideas! Don't ask kids what they want to be when they grow up. Instead, ask them what problems they want to solve.

This changes the conversation from "Whom do I want to work for?" to "What do I need to learn to be able to succeed?"

We can also change over time—for example, before I had kids, I would get a little annoyed at those colleagues who talked incessantly about their kids. In fact, I would often feel like saying, "I believe you are confusing me with someone who cares a lot about your kids!" However, after having kids, I find myself doing *exactly* the same thing. Why do we do it? Well, the kids are always front and center in our minds.

As much as I know that it is inadvisable, I find it wonderful that we can almost live our lives again vicariously through our children. For example, when I was younger, there were many toys and games I would have loved to own but didn't for various reasons. Being able to get these games and toys (or something similar) for my kids makes me feel fantastic. I can guarantee my kids will get toys and games every Christmas, some of which they will like, and others they will not. But Daddy will always be happy!

As a final note on the importance of kids—they will make you stronger, as you will have to lead by example. As a parent, you will need to model the kind of behaviour that you wish to see in your kids. I believe H. Jackson Brown Jr. put it best when he said, "Live so that when your children think of fairness, caring, and integrity, they think of you." Truer words have never been spoken. I've learned that it's very easy to say the right things, but infinitely harder to actually do all of these things yourself. I can easily tell my kids to be nice, to be fair, to treat people with respect, to work hard, to learn more, and so on. But my words won't mean anything if they don't see me doing those same things on a daily basis. They will end up **doing as I did, rather than what I said**.

THE IMPORTANCE OF FRIENDS

> *"A real friend is one who walks in when the rest of the world walks out."*
>
> —WALTER WINCHELL

The world can sometimes seem a lonely place. Even with a supportive family, it can seem that others simply do not understand you or just don't realize what you are going through. This is where friends come in. We usually have no say about our family makeup in our early years, but our friends can evolve in several directions. In my experience, when you are younger, it's the quantity of friends that matters most. Being able to say "Hi" and acknowledge people you know in different situations (school, neighborhood, sports, etc.) boosts self-confidence and makes children feel popular and important. When you grow older, it's much more about the quality of friendships. In fact, I believe you would be super lucky to have more than three really good friends in your entire life. In this context, when considering how successful you really are, you may want to count friends rather than money, because every good friend is priceless. With your best friends, you can do anything or nothing, and it really doesn't matter; you will still have the best of times.

Good friends will make deep marks on your very existence. A true friend never gets in your way, unless of course you are going down. You never really leave the friends you love. You take part of them with you, and you leave part of you behind. Good friends can be incredibly supportive. **Friends are those wonderful people who know all about you and *still* like you.** Truly great friends are hard to find, difficult to leave, and impossible to forget. Using a mathematical analogy: good friends will help *multiply* the happiness in life and help *divide* the sadness. But you should choose your friends wisely. How do you know if a potential friend is right for you?

One concept that has helped me enormously is the idea of identifying how your energy feels after being with people. Some people are energy *givers,* and others are energy *sappers*. If you spend time with some people, they make you feel wonderful. You leave them thinking the world is a better place, and they fill you with optimism, positivity, and clarity. These energy givers are exceedingly good for your psyche and will help you achieve anything that is important to you.

With other people, just spending a little time with them robs you of your energy. You feel tired, pessimistic, negative, and down. Try to spend more time with those who give you energy. Be aware of how you feel after you spend time with people—do you feel invigorated or drained? If you feel tired, then maybe you shouldn't be spending so much time with that person, even if you are close friends for various reasons. Note, people are not absolute energy givers or sappers for everyone. There may be someone who gives you a lot of energy but saps it from others. Likewise, people can sometimes be an energy giver at times and an energy sapper at others. Just go with how they make you feel the majority of time, and mindfulness is key to recognizing the patterns.

THE IMPORTANCE OF SHORTCUTS

When we have issues with people or situations around us, our problems can often be attributed to the *shortcuts* that we use. We need shortcuts to make sense of the world around us. Without these shortcuts we would be completely lost. A good example of shortcuts in action is the notion of first impressions. Why are first impressions so important? It is often said that you never get a second chance to make a first impression. When we meet someone for the first time, we usually make up our minds in just thirty seconds. We think to ourselves: "Yep, I have met people like you before; I have seen this kind of personality before," and we stick to these initial impressions unless we get a big piece of new information. We call this concept getting *anchored*, that is, the first bit of information you see has a disproportionate influence on the rest of your assessment of a situation. Why do we behave in this way? We simply do not have the time and energy to get to know everyone that we meet at a deep level, and so we *have* to anchor to make decisions (e.g., is this person worth spending more time with?).

Your shortcuts help you interpret the world around you. However, your shortcuts can also be misinformed, inaccurate, misleading, or just plain wrong. For example, if someone does not hold a door open for you when you are behind them, that may lead you to believe that this person is rude and selfish. They may, however, believe that holding the door is chauvinistic, or they simply did not see you. Your shortcut to believing this person is rude or selfish may be wildly off the mark, but your behaviour and response will be according to your shortcut. So, are your shortcuts helping you or hindering you? When you think of friends, what are the shortcuts that you use to determine if they are being nice or nasty? Are your shortcuts even accurate?

Finally, remember that no matter what you do, there will be those around you whom you just need to move on from. There are some people that will not listen no matter what, and they will not serve any purpose in your life. A fool of sufficient magnitude can be found to overcome any foolproof system. I am a fan of giving people one chance. We all make mistakes, and it's OK to suffer when one is made that hurts you. However, if the same person does the same thing again and again, then you have to make a change. Fool me once, shame on you. Fool me twice, shame on me.

To have anything come into your life, you have to make space for it. Nature detests a vacuum and usually rushes to fill any kind of void. If you want new clothes, you have to get rid of the old ones that you never wear, first. To get new friends, you have to let go of those who are not helpful to your life, first. Remember, we are not all perfect, and sometimes we need some introspection. Buddha reminds us:

> *"It is easy to see the faults of others, but difficult to see one's own faults. One shows the faults of others like chaff winnowed in the wind, but one conceals one's own faults as a cunning gambler conceals his dice."*
>
> **—BUDDHA**

HOW TO MAINTAIN AND GROW FRIENDSHIPS

> *"Be who you are and say what you feel, because those who mind don't matter and those who matter don't mind."*
>
> **—DR. SEUSS**

Given family is crucial to so many parts of your life, and that friends are the family that you choose, we will examine how to maintain and grow these relationships. My first piece of advice is to understand the trade-off between *quantity* and *quality* time together. Contrary to popular belief, it is not just quality time you want to spend with those that you love. Try gathering people close to you and say to them, "Hey, let's all have some quality time!" The problem is that not everyone will be in the right mood or mind space to enjoy what you perceive to be "quality time." Instead, you want to try and get as much *quantity* time together.

When you have, say, an evening free with each other, you can be spontaneous and go in whatever direction you like (stay at home, cook a meal, play a game, go out, etc.). The magic of deepening a relationship by having a great time together comes naturally when you give it enough time to develop, but it may not come when you are trying to force everyone to have a great *quality* time. In particular, spend *quality* time at work or school (that is, get things done and do not waste time) so that you have more *quantity* time with friends and family (more on this in our chapter on Money and Work).

A quick caution about mixing friends with money. Should you borrow from or lend a friend a significant amount of money? In my experience, it is best to leave this as a last resort. I would rather borrow from a bank (if possible) than from a friend, because with the bank, there is no emotion involved in our relationship. If you lend money to a friend, you might just end up losing both!

Don't let a small dispute get in the way of a great relationship. You should never feel that you owe your good friends anything. Good friends do not owe or keep score, but rather, they help because they want to help. No one is perfect, so make allowance for your friends' imperfections as readily as you do for your own. Focus on what you *like* in other people, not what you dislike. **Everyone has faults and flaws, but the more you focus on what is good in other people, the happier you will be**. The greatest compliment you can pay to others is to demonstrate how thrilled you are to be in their presence.

There are some things in life that we can control, and some things that we cannot. People come in and out of your life all of the time. For example, you may have known some people really well five years ago, but now, you do not even know where they are. **The secret is to try and hold on to the really good people you meet and make a big effort to stay in touch.** In today's über-connected world, there really is no excuse not to keep in touch with those who mean a lot to you. Friends can be like balloons—once you let them go, you may never get them back. But even with best efforts, you will, whether you like it or not, be unable to maintain some friendships. In these cases, it's probably best to believe that there is a very good reason why they were in your life for a period of time, and a very good reason as to why they will not make it into your future.

Making new friends is advisable, but don't forget to **cherish the old ones.** Your job won't take care of you when you are sick, but your friends will. Stay in touch and respect them highly, remembering that respect is a two-way street. You want to live so that your friends can defend you, but never need to. **The only way to have a friend is to be one,** so remember, you reap what you sow. If you neglect people around you or take them for granted, your actions will inevitably catch up with you by distancing yourself from the people who are important.

Sometimes, things will go wrong. If you make a mistake, make sure you apologize immediately, and make sure it is genuine. A bad apology is worse than no apology. A good apology is like an antibiotic; a bad apology is like rubbing salt into the wound. When you are really angry at a friend or family member, step back, calm down, and imagine how you would feel at their funeral. I know this sounds a little morbid, but when you reframe your perspective, you see the world through different eyes. As Charlie Chaplin said, "Life is a tragedy when seen in close-up, but a comedy in long shot."

When you are with people who agree with you, you will experience comfort. Too much comfort, on the other hand, can stunt your growth, because you lose the desire to learn more or explore alternatives that may be enlightening. When you spend time with people who don't agree with you, their different perspective will typically help you grow, since you will consider alternative angles and ways of thinking that help you go deeper and form a more holistic understanding. Balance is key (you don't want to be too comfortable or always challenged to the extreme), and a happy life fluctuates between growth and enjoyment of that growth.

On this vein of dynamism and how your life changes over time, I had a coming-of-age moment with my daughter when she was about ten years old and we discussed swearing. As much as I know that swearing is not appropriate, sometimes it just seems like the perfect way to describe or react to a situation. I realized that up to the age of about ten, we can make the world a very black and white place for our kids. "Always tell the truth—no matter what." "It's never OK to swear." And so on. However, when they grow up a little, we have to introduce them to various anomalies and contradictions. Swearing is never *normally* OK. Maybe sometimes you should just keep your mouth shut.

If you are too blunt, you may be telling the truth, but it can hurt people. For example, if a really large stranger joins you in a conversation, you would not say, "Hey buddy, it's probably best that you lose a few pounds." Why not—you're just being truthful, are you not? Well yes, but you are simultaneously offending this person for no reason, and so it simply is not appropriate. When it comes to family, white lies are sometimes the best thing in the big picture. Being economical with the truth is also sometimes the wisest choice. I have found our ability to discern what to say (and what not to say) comes with experience, and more so, making mistakes along the way.

To get to know people better, you must take more of an interest in them. Lisa Kirk got it right when she said, "A gossip is one who talks to you about others, a bore is one who talks to you about himself, and a brilliant conversationalist is one who talks to you about yourself." Genuinely show that you understand and want to get to know others better, and they will open themselves up, because we all want to be heard and acknowledged.

Can you change people around you? In my experience, it is almost impossible to fundamentally change anyone (outside of your spouse and kids). A good rule of thumb to follow is to never *underestimate* your power to change yourself, and never *overestimate* your power to change others. It's very difficult to commit to the time and patience needed to change anyone at a deep level. Do not waste time trying, and instead try to **accept people for who they are,** and remember you can decide whether you want to maintain a relationship with them.

Changing the minds of people sometimes needs "earthquakes" to occur. For example, traditional parents may never understand why kids want such different things. The "earthquake," unfortunately, is usually a very bad circumstance. People who can master controlled earthquakes (that is, dramatically changing their views without an external event being the motivation) can persuade anyone. Again, you should be mindful of how you spend your time. Don't fight small and petty people. Fighting them brings you down to their size, and they will then beat you with experience. Think bigger than that.

To conclude this chapter, I would like to use a powerful quote to emphasize the importance of friendship:

> *"I think if I've learned anything about friendship, it's to hang in, stay connected, fight for them, and let them fight for you. Don't walk away, don't be distracted, don't be too busy or tired, don't take them for granted. Friends are part of the glue that holds life and faith together."*
>
> **—JON KATZ**

SUMMARY AND KEY LEARNING POINTS

- Having a strong and happy home life with family will help you prepare for anything the world throws at you.
- Children can help complete you because they take you through ranges of emotions and challenges that are difficult to replicate otherwise.
- Watch out for energy *sappers*. Spend more time with energy *givers*.
- Friends are the family that you choose. You can't judge people by their relatives, but you can tell a lot about someone from the friends they choose to keep.
- Shortcuts are essential to interpret and survive the world around us. Being more aware of the shortcuts you developed as you grew and adjusting them deliberately can make you more optimistic and foster closer relationships.
- You have to actively work on your relationships to keep them healthy. Like anything, relationships can become stale.
- You need to move on from those who are not helping you with your life to make space for those who will help you grow.
- Concentrate on spending quantity time (as opposed to quality time) with those you cherish.
- Try not to mix friends with money. You may end up losing both.
- Frame situations and interactions in your relationships in ways that help you rather than hold you

back; a little perspective goes a long way to make you feel better.

- It is almost impossible to fundamentally change people around you—don't waste time trying to do so, and accept people for who they are.

Exercises

TRUST, ENERGY, AND MAINTAINING RELATIONSHIPS

The purpose of this exercise is to make you more aware of the close people around you and how they help shape your experiences and views.

Make a list of all the people that you truly trust. This can include family members (both close and far), friends, neighbors, teachers, colleagues, teammates, or anyone else that means a lot to you.

For each of these people, complete the following sections:

- **Why**—Make a list of all of the reasons why you like this person (to remind you of why they are in your life in the first place).

- **Trust**—On a scale of 1 to 10, how much do you really trust them?

  A 10 would mean that you completely trust them with all of your secrets and, in effect, your life. A 1 would mean that you trust them a little but always have to be very careful what you say in front of them, usually because they have broken your trust in the past.

- **Energy**—Try to assign a value of between 1 and 10 in terms of how you feel after you spend time with them. For our purposes, let's assume the following: A 10 means the person typically leaves you invigorated, positive about life in general, and extremely optimistic towards your future.

  A 1 means the person leaves you feeling drained, pessimistic, and fearful or apprehensive towards your future.

- **Maintenance**—How hard have you tried to maintain or strengthen this relationship within the past year?

  A 10 means you are constantly there for this person and have gone way over and above in keeping the relationship healthy. You do things (unrequested) regularly for this person, you talk with each other constantly, and they are never far from your thoughts.

  A 1 means you have neglected this person and cannot remember the last nice thing you did for them.

This exercise will help you understand not only who really matters to you but also whether or not you are cultivating the relationship to brighten your future. The exercise may also point out people whom you perhaps should not be spending so much time with. Most people have never really taken the time to think about these dimensions and have instead let their relationships evolve, without intervention, over time. As you grow older, you will realize more and more that your time is finite, and you will have to make decisions as to where you spend your time.

PEER GROUP

Think about the people that you spend the most time with outside of your immediate family and colleagues (if you are working). This peer group will typically be a social group that is made up of people with similar interests and social status and, usually, of similar age. The purpose of your peer group is to share knowledge, discuss problems, and provide guidance and perspective to face the wider world.

For each member of your peer group, assess the individuals on a scale of 1 to 10 (where 1 is not at all, and 10 is completely) along the following four dimensions:

- **Learning**—How much is this member helping me learn new things for my future (by providing insights, finding resources, sharing best practices, and so on)?
- **Encouragement and Accountability**—How much is this member providing support to help me overcome my difficulties and attain new heights while helping me get back on track if I start to get off course?
- **Feeling**—How much does this member help me feel positive about the future?

- **Comfort**—How much does this member make me feel secure in what I am trying to achieve and that I am living a good life?

As a whole, does your peer group help in raising you to new heights? Does it make you feel comfortable? Are you the smartest or most accomplished member of your group?

Peer groups typically evolve organically, and most people will never stop and think about how much of an effect their peer group has on their life. Becoming aware and deliberately deciding to adjust your peer group will help immensely in you being the very best you can be.

SHORTCUTS

Shortcuts are necessary to understand and survive in the world around us. The purpose of this exercise is to understand the shortcuts that you default to. Are your shortcuts keeping you from creating or maintaining quality, fulfilling relationships because you often judge people upon first meeting? Simply becoming more aware of your shortcuts can help tremendously in amending them to help you in your future.

1. Let's start off with your fears. Make a list of all of the things that you are afraid of. (Note: Your list may contain common fears such as heights, the dark, flying, spiders, snakes, dogs, injections, loud noises, being alone, germs, and so on. Your list may also contain people, situations [such as tests or exams], results [such as failure, lack of money],

and other items. Think hard and make sure you capture all of your fears. Do not worry if your list is long—most people have several fears.)

2. For each of your fears, assign a rating of between 1 and 10 (where 1 means you are a little bit apprehensive of this issue, and 10 means you are absolutely petrified and the fear affects your life significantly. For example, you cannot fly at all or cannot go into parks because of a fear of dogs).

3. Take any fear that is greater than 5, and try to distil where the fear came from. Was there an incident when you were younger? Have you always had the fear? Did other people around you influence you or share their fear with you? For example, parents may pass on some of their fears to their children.

4. Consider what people who don't share this fear can do. What would make a considerable difference? What would be an incredible test to prove you have overcome the fear? For example, I have a colleague who had a fear of heights who went bungee jumping to get over his fear. This may be a little extreme, but try to think of as many ways to overcome your fear as possible.

5. Do what you came up with in Step 4.

Step 3 above will help you become aware of the origins of your fears and perhaps provide clues as to how to overcome them. You may think that there is a step missing between Steps 3 and 4. (That is, you understand where the fear came from, and appreciate what it would take to show that you have overcome the fear, but the real question is *how*?)

I have not left out a step. The how can be incredibly complicated and could require lots of time and intervention. The quickest way to establish a new shortcut is simply to do it. For example, when you are nervous about getting into a cold swimming pool, what is the best thing to do? Dip your toes in to ascertain the exact temperature? Wait until you feel different and pluck up enough courage to go in? These measures will only delay what you really have to do. The best action is simply to jump in. When you keep thinking about the issue, your mind will have you in knots. Jumping in gives your mind no choice (and all fear is rooted in the mind). Of course, this giant leap of faith (pun intended) may not be feasible or realistic, but consider it anyway.

Of course, shortcuts are not all about fears, and positive shortcuts can be very helpful. I believe the best way to understand shortcuts is simply to examine your own and be aware of where your mind typically goes. Take a piece of paper and go through the following list one by one, writing what immediately comes to your mind. Don't think about each item—just write your immediate thoughts. After you have completed all words, you can look at what you have written (and even better, compare it to a friend who tries the same exercise) to elicit your shortcuts and how they may affect your thinking.

Happy	Love	Respect	Black
White	Clear	Nice	Nasty
Low	Fear	Hope	Brown
Canada (or your own country)	School	Work	Play
Children	Adults	Study	Worthwhile
Boring	Exciting	Careful	Society
Community	Government	War	Nature

Once you have completed the above, you will have a very good idea of your own shortcuts. Relating these shortcuts back to our chapter topic, try to think about times when shortcuts have damaged a relationship or times when you trusted your shortcut and something amazing happened. The key is simply awareness.

As an aside, marketers are experts in working on your shortcuts and have developed a concept called "mindshare." When you think of various brands or types of goods, what immediately comes to mind? Try the following mini-exercise.

For each of the following, write down what immediately comes to mind when you see the organization. Of paramount importance is what you immediately think, so do not deliberate. You must write down the first things that come to mind.

- McDonald's
- Apple (company)
- Coca-Cola
- Amazon
- Tesla

Look at what you wrote for each answer. It is very likely that the organizations have spent a small fortune in marketing to ensure your mindshare (that is, what you think immediately when you hear these organizations) conforms to what they would like it to be.

For example, for Amazon, many people will write down a subset of the following words: fast, overnight, free delivery, cheap, choice, and so on. The marketing team at Amazon has tried very hard to ensure these are the types of words that come to customers' minds, and therefore, they are the *shortcuts* customers will use when thinking of their brand.

REFLECTION QUESTIONS

- Who helps you most in life? Who are your true friends? Why?
- Who hinders you in any way?
- Do you give enough energy and time to your best friends?
- Are you an optimist or a pessimist? Do you usually see the glass half full or half empty? Do you usually see the problems and faults, or the opportunities and advantages? The more self-aware you are, the more authentic and honest you can be, and you can become a better friend or family member.

CHAPTER 4

HEALTH AND WELL-BEING

"If you are depressed, you are living in the past. If you are anxious, you are living in the future. If you are at peace, you are living in the present."

—LAO TZU, TAO TE CHING

Health is superimportant. As the saying goes, a healthy body means a healthy mind. It is a great shame, however, that it doesn't work the other way around, because I could easily sit around all day reading books to get that six-pack! Take thirty seconds to think about this question: Do you know how to be healthy?

Has there ever been a topic that has garnered as many pieces of advice as to how to get and remain healthy? The problem I find is that there is not only an incredible amount of research and advice given by well-renowned scholars, but in some cases, even they cannot agree on the basics. Is a keto diet OK for you? How about intermittent fasting? Is it OK to have some processed foods? How about going without water for a day? Where do you even begin?

First things first, let's make the universal truths clear. The points below are ubiquitous when it comes to advice on ensuring a healthy body:

- Move or exercise frequently;
- eat well by concentrating on fresh, high-quality foods such as fruits and vegetables, and avoiding or limiting processed foods such as cookies and chips;
- don't do anything to excess (including consuming any type of food or drink);
- rest well and get good-quality sleep;
- cut down on things that hurt the body, such as stress, bad diets, drugs, alcohol, and so on; and
- get plenty of fresh air.

These points are fairly obvious when you think about them, and they give you the basics of how to get and stay healthy. But what do you do beyond that? Depending on whom you listen to, there are numerous diets, ways of thinking, and best practices that will lead to a healthy life. I have found that experimenting yourself is the only way to really elicit what works best for you. We are all different, and outside of the fundamentals listed above, it is difficult to know what will work well or not so well for ourselves. Smoking has been widely criticized to cause a plethora of health problems, yet we know of centenarians who have smoked all of their lives.

Our variety of genes and history ensure that there is no one-size-fits-all, so you need to try out what works best for yourself. In this chapter, I will share with you what I have found to help lead to a healthier life. Hopefully you will learn a number of tips that will help you in your future, and I encourage you to keep an open mind, try different approaches, and simply **listen to your body and be mindful of how you feel.** Your body will tell you what works.

Remember, being healthy and fit are more than just personal goals—they are **valuable gifts that we give to the people around us.** Being fit and feeling great will ensure that we're there for everyone. It makes us better spouses, parents, siblings, and friends. **When you feel great, you will go over and above for those around you.** When you don't feel good or have low energy, you will not be able to do everything you wish. Anyone who has lived with a very sick person will know just how much it takes out of you to look after them. Health is so important and a top priority for a happy life—even if you make billions of dollars, you will find it demanding to be happy without good health.

FOOD AND DRINK

One of the anomalies in life is that most things that taste delicious are not necessarily good for you (junk food, for example). These processed foods have been deliberately designed to appeal to your taste buds (and various psychological weaknesses) to apparently satisfy your cravings. However, there are many, many exceptions to this rule—many types of fruit, for example. Make these exceptions the majority of your diet. Fruits and vegetables are fantastic because they give you so much energy and nutrients with minimal taxing of your digestive system. Try to have as many as possible in a day, and substitute where possible for negative foods, such as having a salad instead of the fries. Put simply, eat more foods that grow on trees and plants and eat less food that is manufactured in a plant.

Diets can work in helping you lose weight, but they typically only work in the short term. As soon as you get off them, you return quickly to your prior state. **You want to find ways of eating and drinking that are sustainable in the long term.**

Alcohol, like most things, can be OK in moderation, but the more you have, the worse it gets. If you can, cut it out completely, but at the very least, cut down consumption. Every bit helps. The reason that alcohol can be difficult to cut down on is the fact that it has permeated so many parts of our society. When it was illegal and there was only moonshine or other similar homemade beverages available, cutting it down was simpler. Now, it is hard to find a good restaurant, party, special occasion, travel option, or similar situation that does *not* serve alcohol. It has become the norm. With the normality, large organizations have realized how to appeal to as wide a market as possible. This is why your options to consume alcohol have come a long way from the moonshine days. With coolers of all kinds; red, white, pink, and sparkling wines; an astonishing array of beers and ciders; and spirits/liquors too numerous to count, there is something for everyone.

A similar trend has occurred with cannabis, which is already legal in many parts of Canada and the United States—and the acceptance continues to expand. Because of the legality, organizations have figured out many ways to make the product appealing to as wide an audience as possible. Long gone are the days of dodgy drug dealers selling small amounts of cannabis for users to mould to their liking. Walking into a cannabis store, you will be greeted with prerolls, edibles, pipes, bongs, vape pens, and many more ideas to help you get high. Like alcohol, the best way is to cut it out completely, especially because of all of the acid that is introduced into your body to rob you of health. But even if you cannot resist, the less the better, and remember that it is not helping you achieve optimum health.

Be careful of marketing ploys that surround us to make more money for the instigators. For example, the dairy industry has brainwashed billions of people towards the importance and necessity of dairy products. Mothers' milk is good for babies, but after that, the importance of dairy products has been vastly overstated. Try what you like, and consider how it affects your body. Do you feel better or worse after you have consumed something?

Detoxify yourself regularly. There are many supplements and pieces of advice (such as intermittent fasting) that will help you get rid of the accumulated toxins in your system. Your body wants to be clean and healthy, and detoxing lets it get better naturally and faster than you can possibly imagine. Personally, I try to eat regular food (outside of fruit) only between the hours of 11:00 a.m. and 6:00 p.m. This gives my body plenty of time during the day and night to digest, assimilate, and clean itself. Do you notice how tired you feel after having a big meal? Why is that? It is because your body is expending so much energy to try and digest all of that food. Do you like eating? If so, here is a secret to allow you to eat a lot. Eat less. Why? Because then you will live long and healthy enough to eat a lot! It's been said to look after your stomach for your first fifty years, and it will look after you for your next fifty years. Wonderful advice for staying and feeling healthy.

For your diet, try to limit your intake of the three whites—refined flour, sugar, and salt. A little bit of each will not do too much harm, but we typically go to excess on at least one of them. Try to systematically reduce the three whites in your diet. Don't add salt to your food if you can help it. Don't add sugar to your coffee or tea. Try to stay away from cookies, pastries, cakes, muffins, white bread, certain cereals, pizzas, and so on. Do not drink any kind of fizzy drink or juice with added sugar. I realize this may require a seismic shift in your eating habits, but try to console yourself knowing that you are on the way to a far healthier body. It will become easier when you start to see results, and, more importantly, when you feel appreciably more energy.

About 71 percent of the earth's surface is covered in water.[*] Up to 60 percent of the human adult body is water.[†] The brain and heart are composed of about 73 percent water, and your lungs are about 83 percent water. Your skin contains 64 percent water, your muscles and kidneys are about 79 percent water, and even your bones are fairly watery at 31 percent.[‡] You can survive two to three months without food, but without water you would

---

* Water Science School, "How Much Water is There on Earth?", U.S. Geological Survey, November 13, 2019, https://www.usgs.gov/water-science-school/science/how-much-water-there-earth

† Allie Mahowald (RDN), "Water: Essential for Your Body," Hometown Health: Speaking of Health, Mayo Clinic Health System, September 29, 2022, https://www.mayoclinichealthsystem.org/hometown-health/speaking-of-health/water-essential-to-your-body-video

‡ Peter Morales-Brown, "What Percentage of the Human Body Is Water?" Medical News Today, last updated November 3, 2025, https://www.medicalnewstoday.com/articles/what-percentage-of-the-human-body-is-water

struggle to last a week.[§] Needless to say, your body absolutely depends on water to survive!

Every cell, tissue, and organ in your body needs water to work properly. Water can come from the food you eat, especially fresh fruit, yogurt, soups, and so on, but primarily comes from the fluids you drink. According to research from *Medical Daily*, an estimated 75 percent of Americans suffer from chronic dehydration.[¶] Drinking lots of water is not only necessary to survive but to ensure you can attain optimal health. My simple advice is to have a big glass of water every morning to start the day right. Thereafter, try to drink at least eight normal glasses of water a day. Try to cut out other forms of fluids and substitute them for water. Other fluids have their own repercussions (such as extra calories, mood altering affects, diuretic natures, etc.), so just stick to plain water.

Occasional indulgence in food or drink can be OK. As the saying goes, life is too short to drink bad wine. It's only when you go to excess that problems are likely. Restraint not only leads to a healthier body but also helps train other skills crucial to life, such as discipline and strength of will. Finally, don't go grocery shopping when you are hungry. You increase your chances of overspending today and then overeating tomorrow.

Given the overwhelming literature out there on nutrition, if you are looking for just one book to help you understand and apply lessons to your nutrition to make you feel better and live longer, I

---

§ Natalie Silver, "How Long Can You Live Without Food?" Healthline, medically reviewed by Megan Soliman, MD, updated January 19, 2024, https://www.healthline.com/health/food-nutrition/how-long-can-you-live-without-food

¶ John Ericson, "75% of Americans May Suffer From Chronic Dehydration, According to Doctors," Medical Daily, July 3, 2013, https://www.medicaldaily.com/75-americans-may-suffer-chronic-dehydration-according-doctors-247393

would recommend *Good Energy: The Surprising Connection Between Metabolism and Limitless Health,* by Calley and Casey Means. The book does an excellent job of explaining the science behind using food and drink to optimize your health, well-being, and chances of living longer and happier. Be warned: It will likely challenge some of your fundamental beliefs towards what we put in our body!

LEARNING FROM OTHERS

> *"Anger is an acid that can do more harm to the vessel in which it is stored than to anything on which it is poured."*
>
> **—MAHATMA GANDHI**

How you look at people around you and frame their behaviour in your own mind will go a long way to determining how you feel. If you want to feel healthy and vibrant and alive, this topic of viewing others cannot be ignored. As Gandhi reminded us, anger towards someone usually does far more damage to the person getting angry then the supposed target of that anger. In many cases, the other person may not be aware (or care at all) about your anger towards them. The person getting angry will feel their blood pressure rise, possibly do damage to their internals, and most of all, lose the calmness from which good things tend to originate. Anger can be helpful in some cases (for example, when anger at yourself making mistakes drives you to make long-lasting changes for the better) but generally is not a positive emotion to feel regularly. Depression comes from anger without enthusiasm.

Think positively, and where possible, assume positive intentions. For example, if you really have no way of ever finding out someone's motives for doing something, why be negative or cynical by assuming they acted with ulterior motives? Instead, if you have no way of ever verifying, then assume they had sound reasons and acted in good faith. This makes no difference to the situation, or to the other person, but makes a lot of difference where it really counts—in your own heart and soul.

What's more important when you are deciding which clothes to wear? Looking good or feeling good? It's a bit of a trick question because one is a subset of the other. Why do you want to look good? Because it makes you feel great! It's all about the feeling really. A better question would be, do you prefer looks or comfort? To which I always say comfort, as anyone in my classes will attest! Keep in mind that of all the things you wear, your expression is the most important.

HEALING AND A BETTER QUALITY OF LIFE

Your body is the best natural healer that you could possibly wish for. It is the most amazing chemist that you will ever find. Our bodies have figured out the solutions to nearly every disease possible over the millions of years of animal evolution. We are still evolving and need help in some key areas, most notably cancer, heart disease, neurological ailments such as Alzheimer's disease, and diabetes. There has been a significant interest in longevity, and not only living longer lives, but more importantly, living healthier lives. My favorite book on this topic is *Outlive: The Science and Art of Longevity*, and I highly recommend you read this book to get a grip on what may happen in your life from a health perspective and what to do right now to help you in your future years.

One of the fundamental tenets of this book (and much similar literature and podcasts) is the desire to live not only longer but also healthier lives. As the author puts it, we (the scientific and medical community) have done a fantastic job of lengthening lives and helping people survive longer when afflicted with these major diseases, but not such a good job in **preventing them in the first place**. I want to live a long life, but I do not want to spend my final ten to twenty years in and out of hospital, enduring endless appointments, having to put up with constant mental and physical hardship, and becoming a burden to those around me. Is that really the quality of life that will make me and others around me happy? So the question becomes, what can you do to get better if you are sick, and to give yourself the best chance of enjoying your twilight years without problems with your health getting in the way?

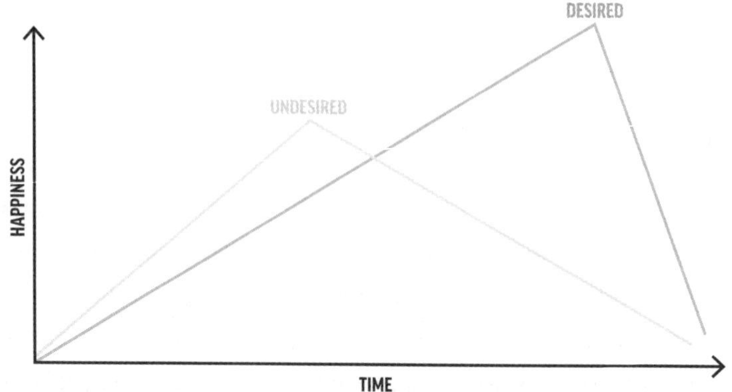

Quite simply, I advise taking as little medication as possible. Sometimes it is necessary, and of course if you need medication for a serious illness, then by all means take it. However, do not reach for Advil, Tylenol, ibuprofen, acetaminophen, cough syrup, and so on as the immediate solution. You are putting more toxins in your body and weakening your immune system. Let your body naturally fight off as much as possible. Every time you take any kind of medicine, your body gets a little more used to it and builds tolerance, and the effects will likely fade over time so that you will have to take more to get the same advantage. Why not save that effect for when you really need it? Again, if you must take medicine for some reason, then absolutely go ahead. Just don't reach for it automatically when the pain or symptoms are not strong—give your body a chance to get stronger.

I learned the power of minimizing medicine from my parents. They grew up in small villages in India, and when they were younger, they rarely took medicine for anything. The reason wasn't because they wanted to strengthen their bodies but because there was very little on offer from the local doctor/pharmacy. In essence, there were two options. You either took a massive pill or an injection, which pretty much knocked you out for a couple of days. The intention was forced rest, which would hopefully result in you waking up better. Note, the medicine didn't actually attack the root cause of any illness, but instead, just sedated you to stop the pain. Unfortunately, some people didn't wake up from this sedation. This led to few people wanting to take any medicine and only reserving it for emergencies, when there was little other choice. Because of the situation, my parents rarely took any medicine, and instead relied on their bodies to fight off minor issues.

The concept hit home when I observed that in forty years of living and working in England, I hardly ever saw my parents not go to work because of sickness. Sure, they got the same minor colds, headaches, and issues that others got, but they were never bad enough to miss work. If my father had the flu, he would shiver a little and have the sniffles, but would still go to his labour job and finish the day. I concluded that the lack of medicine when growing up forced their immune system to naturally grow tougher, which helped them deal with future such issues. Try to make your immune system stronger by letting it work and by not reaching for medication quickly. The first few times you get a cold may seem difficult, but the long-term benefits are worth it, and things will get easier.

If you are diagnosed with an illness, consider the following. Doctors are trained to give advice based on past statistics. **Never accept a negative prognosis**. Think positively, and truly believe that you will get better, and you more likely will. There are countless examples of individuals defying the odds and recovering from illnesses where they were initially given no chance.

William Glasser wrote, "What happened in the past that was painful has a great deal to do with what we are today." Personally, I can attest to these words by thinking of how pain has played a huge role in making me who I am today. To date, I have had eleven surgeries on my eyes (three transplants and many laser surgeries). From a young age, I had to get used to wearing hard contact lenses to deal with my condition of keratoconus. Wearing these lenses was painful, irritating (to keep up with the daily routine of cleaning and dealing with copious infections), and frustrating. I remember after my first transplant spending three days in hospital recovering and taking nonstop pain medication, and then having to wear sunglasses for the following month and barely being able to leave my home. However, the experiences taught me key skills to help in my life, most notably pain management, discipline, perspective, gratitude, and faith that you can get through anything.

Everyone deals with pain differently. It's hard to be 100 percent empathetic because we never quite know everything that someone is going through at any given time. The best we can do is imagine how the pain might feel to ourselves, and then assume that others will feel the same way. The wonderful Athenian poet Solon captured this idea beautifully in the early sixth century BC when he wrote:

"If all men were to bring their miseries together in one place, most would be glad to take each his own home again rather than take a portion out of the common stock."

My three go-to methods for trying to deal with pain without resorting to medication (where possible) are distraction, belief, and perspective.

Our minds are usually racing along at breakneck speeds, just looking for things to focus on. Whatever we focus on typically takes up our attention at the expense of other sensations (unless they signal an emergency, such as a fire or dangerous situation). Whenever you are deep into something, like a hobby or anything that is totally encapsulating your attention, you will often not notice simple messages to your body, such as the need to eat or sleep. Your mind is distracted. To realize the power of distraction, look into how so much of magic works. The magician sends your attention one way while performing a sleight of hand that is now unnoticed given the distraction.

What should you distract your mind with? Anything that you can get lost in. Books, movies, TV shows, magazines, etc., all work well. My favorites are comedies, because they not only provide fantastic distraction but also a nice dose of natural chemicals such as endorphins, dopamine, and serotonin that help tremendously to deal with the pain. I also find anything that really forces you to think will help in distraction. For example, trying to plan, in fine detail, my next holiday.

Positive beliefs can be wonderful in making you feel better.

Consider if your predominant beliefs—what goes through your mind the most—are helping or hindering you. I like to believe the following:

- I believe my body is getting better;
- I believe my body is figuring out the best way to get better quickly and permanently;
- I believe I will be back to normal quickly; and
- I believe this pain is temporary and, like all things, will subside.

Finally, a bit of perspective always helps me to alleviate the feelings of pain. Like most parents, I have spent considerable time in waiting rooms for many children's doctors and specialists for my kids. When entering these rooms, I'm usually praying in my mind that my child is OK and that no significant procedure is needed. However, I find that when I'm leaving these rooms, I'm usually very grateful that my child does not have a serious or advanced condition. I'm not sure if this is a good way to feel, but I find that it's almost impossible not to make comparisons, and being surrounded by people who are in worse states than yourself does, in some way, make you feel better.

You can use this knowledge to try and help frame conditions with a more positive mindset. Simply understanding that things could be worse can be very helpful. There are optimists among us who can be surprising because they always seem to see the glass half full, even when emotions and conditions are making everyone else frustrated. These optimists are, I believe, among the very best healers that we have available. They have a natural ability to make people feel better by reminding us of what is possible, both positive and negative.

Pain is never easy to deal with, and it can be horrible to experience directly or to see loved ones go through. Medication can help, and it's also worth adding as many natural tools to your arsenal to help deal with pain. Distracting yourself through immersion into alternative thoughts, maintaining positive beliefs, and getting a helpful perspective are three such tools. I encourage you to think about and add more that resonate and work for you.

EXERCISE AND REST

You cannot relax your way to happiness. Happiness comes as a result of doing. Try to exercise first thing in the morning or early in the day. Not only do you reap the rewards to feel great all day, but you also cannot find excuses to not exercise later in the day. If you plan to exercise late in the day, there are a million things that may happen before then to get in your way. The earlier you exercise, the less chance there is for something to prevent you from doing so.

There is a famous saying from Norman Schwarzkopf that states, "The more you sweat in peace, the less you bleed in war." Most exercise is completed in private and will make you feel better in all parts of your life. Sports are incredibly powerful, because they allow you to lose yourself in the game and competition and not notice (directly) how the sport is improving your health. (William James eloquently reminds us of the opposite by stating, "Boredom results from being attentive to the passage of time itself.") If you go for an hour run on a treadmill, you better have some good music or be watching something interesting, because otherwise it can get really boring really quickly. This is another reason why running or walking outside is nicer—the changes in scenery and nature help alleviate boredom and take your mind off the exertion required.

The mind is the most complex and powerful tool in the world. Use it wisely, and it can push through barriers you never thought possible. For example, even the thought of running a marathon will exhaust most people. Running just half a mile will cause many to be out of breath, and completing just over twenty-six miles seems like a world away. However, with enough training, discipline, patience, and endeavour, almost all of us can work up to this seemingly impossible feat.

At the end of every day, you want to be what is considered a "good" tired. This can come from several aspects—good physical workouts, working hard to achieve goals, having lots of energetic fun, helping others, and so on—but not too much from stress. Looking for this state will help in getting a better night's sleep, which in turn gives you a great start to tomorrow morning. At the opposite end of the spectrum from exercise is the importance of rest. If you have a "good" tired at the end of a day, your sleep should be deeper and more refreshing.

Do you like to sleep? So do I. But you must realize that if you want your dreams to come true, you must not oversleep. Get the minimum number of hours required (for most people this is eight, but some people need less), but not much more than that. If you get into the habit of getting up late, you will miss out on many opportunities. When I was about thirteen, I received a piece of advice from a successful uncle who informed me, "There is plenty of time to sleep when you die." Luckily, the amount of sleep that you need typically decreases as you get older, but I don't know a single self-made successful person who sleeps a lot.

If you want to give anything up (vice/addiction/bad habit), concentrate on what you want and not on what you want to stop. Give energy to what you want to replace the vice with. Our minds cannot tell if something is good or bad, so focus on the positive (how you will feel when successful), rather than the negative habit you are trying to kick. You are still dealing with the same situation but have reframed it to make success more probable. Remember, you always wish you stuck with your diet when you are waiting to see your doctor.

Where possible, try to breathe through your nose instead of through your mouth. James Nestor has written a fantastic book called *Breath: The New Science of a Lost Art*, and he provides some wonderful advice on how to more effectively do the one thing we all do so many times a day: breathe.

BALANCE

At this point, I would like to discuss the term "balance." We talk a lot about the need for balance in our lives. Work-life balance and family-life balance are common terms we look to strive for. In reality, I have found that **to achieve a lot, you have to get used to sacrificing along the way**. The key is not just balance, but rather, *long-term* balance. It is hard to be balanced in just one day, or even in one week or one month. Try having a balanced day, where you spend equal amounts of time and energy on work or school, home, family, friends, exercise, and so on. It is more than a little difficult to achieve. Instead, think of balance as being in the long term. You may choose to spend most of this month concentrating on your study or your work. You may choose to take it a little easier in December and spend more time with family and friends. The balance can be attained in the long run.

More broadly, I believe that this is what life is really all about. You have a number of levers that you can push forward at any time, with the main ones being relationships with loved ones, family, and friends; health and well-being; work, leadership, or business; and learning or study. Realistically, you cannot push all of these levers at the same time. **Life is really about deciding which levers to push and when, as well as to what degree**. We may not consciously do this, but that's what life is all about. You have to make decisions and trade-offs. Of course, there are consequences to everything. For example, it may be possible to leave your work/career levers aside for a while, but if you neglect them too much, you may feel unfulfilled and broke. You may be able to leave your relationship levers alone for a while, but if you do so too much, then you may have problems later on in life.

THE POWER OF WALKING

Movement is essential to life, and every healthy program encourages you to move around as much as possible. Running is fantastic, but unfortunately for me, I experienced some serious back and knee injuries in my early thirties that prevent me from running. Therefore, I decided to take up walking and have never looked back. In my world, walking is the very best of exercises. It burns lots of calories and can help you lose weight, yet is not so hard on your body that it can't be kept up for long periods. When walking outside you feel closer to nature, and there is no better way to explore some areas than simply walking around. **Getting close to nature is a great way to clear your mind.** Appreciate the mountains, rocks, water, fields—it will bring an inner calm that is hard to find elsewhere.

When I visit a city or area that I have never been to before, I tend to split up the surrounding area into regions that I can walk every day. Even though long walks may prove tiring, you rarely feel exhausted like you may after a vigorous run or bike ride. Walking costs almost nothing (just remember to invest in some great shoes), and almost invariably makes you feel better with the fresh air and break from other parts of your life.

Walking also makes it easier to get to know your community and stop and talk to those you pass regularly. That's much harder to do when biking or running since you are travelling so fast and do not want to slow or stop because you are looking for that powerful workout. My walks have reminded me that people change over time. Where I live, there are many great trails, and I enjoy the walks immensely. When I first moved here, there was a clear pattern on how people interacted with you on the trails. Anyone over about the age of twenty-five would say, "Hi," stop for a quick conversation, or at the very least, acknowledge your presence. However, anyone younger than that would invariably walk right past without even a hint of acknowledgement. It would make me think, *Wow, the younger generation is so different, and we are losing the basic skills of com-*

munication and community. However, I see those same people now, and they are in very different stages of their lives. Now, they wave enthusiastically!

Do you know what Aristotle, Beethoven, Charles Darwin, Nikola Tesla, and Sigmund Freud all had in common? Yep, you guessed it: They all loved to walk and did so regularly. What a fantastic set of people to learn from. To finish this section and to encourage you to walk more, consider the following piece by theologian and philosopher Søren Kierkegaard on the power of walking:

"Above all, do not lose your desire to walk: every day I walk myself into a state of well-being and walk away from every illness. I have walked myself into my best thoughts, and I know of no thought so burdensome that one cannot walk away from it. Even if one were to walk for one's health and it were constantly one station ahead—I would still say:

Walk!

Besides, it is also apparent that in walking one constantly gets as close to well-being as possible, even if one does not quite reach it—but by sitting still, and the more one sits still, the closer one comes to feeling ill. Health and salvation can be found only in motion ... if one just keeps on walking, everything will be all right."*

MENTAL WELLNESS

The world is moving forward at a lightning-fast speed, and it is difficult for us to keep up with everything that is going on around us. The way technology and marketing have evolved guarantees that we will be distracted constantly. Our need to be constantly moving has contributed to the proliferation of coffee shops around the world, because so many of us were tired and needed something to provide that boost to get through the day. Personally, I hardly ever drank coffee while working in investment banking, but when I came to Canada, I could not resist. It just seemed part of

* Søren Kierkegaard, "Letter to Henrietta Lund," 1847, trans. Henrik Rosenmeier (1978).

the uniform, and I was asked several times a day, "Would you like to meet for coffee?" "Should we discuss over coffee?" or "Let's go for a walk and grab a coffee." Now, I try to limit my intake of coffee to emergencies, but it's astonishing just how much of the drink is consumed globally every day. (As a side note, there are now many more tea shops opening, and I attribute this to people being too excitable or anxious and in need of something to help them calm down!)

Why is meditating so important? Because it increases your ability to stay calm. Many problems and situations arise because people are too emotional, angry, or upset to think rationally. This is why it is so easy for a third party to come in and calm two people in an argument—the third party is not emotionally attached to the issue. Similarly, things like road rage only occur when you get emotional and allow the situation to get the better of you. If you are calm, then rational and sensible thoughts and actions follow. If you are emotional, stressed, or angry, then thoughts and subsequent actions are distorted. Staying calm is not easy, especially in very trying circumstances, but **the calmer you are in life, the happier you will surely become**.

As mentioned in the previous section, I love to walk. My walks are typically about two hours long and take me deep into the beautiful nature surrounding my home and work. What goes through my mind over these two hours? I have developed a ritual which has helped me exceptionally to both make the most out of the walks and look forward to them every day. My ritual for the first hour of the walk is to repeat affirmations in my head. There are many books out there that can help you develop affirmations for yourself, and there is an exercise for you to develop your own affirmations at the end of this chapter. The only people in the world who know what my affirmations entail are my wife and children, so I will not be sharing here. Currently, I have seven that I use, and each is repeated for about nine minutes. Suffice it to say, the more personal you make them, the more likely they will work their wonders on you.

Now I didn't intend for this to happen, but I have realized that repeating the affirmations helps me meditate. Meditation is a wonderful practice, and I encourage you to try through various forms and guidance. Personally, I have found meditation to feel wonderful when it works, but incredibly frustrating because it is so difficult to do. Meditation largely involves trying to quiet the mind so that your thoughts and ego do not cloud what is really happening around you. Although simple in principle, it is incredibly difficult to practice because our minds are so active. Try thinking of nothing for the next thirty seconds. Put this book down and give it a try.

What did you think of? The chances are there were many thoughts going through your mind, and you probably succumbed to at least one of them. Emptying your mind is challenging. Instead, if you repeat affirmations (or a chant or a mantra), you get to almost the same desired peace of meditation but without the struggle to completely empty your mind. You are still focusing your efforts and will get distracted from time to time. However, it is far easier to gently bring your attention back to your affirmation, rather than try to empty your mind completely.

After repeating the affirmations for the first half of my walk, I then let my mind wander for the second half. My mind has already been disciplined with affirmations that I find helpful, and I kid you not, virtually every great idea I have had in the past twenty years has come in the second half of my walks. It's likely a mixture of the fresh air, the movement and increase of blood to all parts of the body, the relaxation from a not-too-vigorous activity, the disciplining of the mind, and the reminders of the affirmations that go deep into my soul that causes the great ideas to come forth.

In the vein of affirmations, don't wait for things unless you really have to. Most people say things like the following when they want a goal: "When I settle down, then I'll ..." "When the time is right, then I'll ..." or "When I finish this part of my life, then I'll ..." The problem with always looking into the future is that it never arrives. Instead, act as if you already have that goal, and then it will come to you faster than you can possibly imagine. If you keep waiting for a time to start (such as in the New Year), chances are you will either never start or give up quickly after starting. The mistake you made was to assume the special time would make a difference, when really the only time to consider is now. Affirmations have multiple benefits, most notably on how you feel about your progress in life and your optimism.

Don't try too hard to suppress emotions; let them run wild in a safe environment (such as the second half of your walk). If you get into the habit of regularly suppressing, you are in fact going against nature. What I do is get some of these emotions out during my walks. I can get quite pent up about things (raising my heartbeats by twenty beats per minute), but I actually feel calmer about the issue afterwards. You need to have sanctuaries in your life where you can get away, reset, and just be yourself. My walks provide me with my sanctuary.

In a similar vein, there is also something great about punching a bag (I have a big standup punch bag in my gym). Punching helps release frustration and anger, which leaves a gap for some peace to enter you. The bottom line is that **life can be seen as a pressure cooker and you need vents to let out steam.** If you don't have enough vents, you will, at the very least, feel overwhelmed, and worse, you will start to miss things and burn yourself out. A large part of your happiness in life depends on the quality of your thoughts, and this includes flushing out the negative ones as well as fostering more positive ones.

MOTIVATION AND STAYING GROUNDED

> *"The only difference between a* rut *and a* grave *are the dimensions."*
>
> —ELLEN GLASGOW [EMPHASIS MINE]

So how do you motivate yourself to do what you should to get and remain healthy? Consider the following:

- Those who get up and work out every morning cannot believe that others do not.
- Those who work out hard for the first time can't believe others actually do this and enjoy it every day.

What is the difference? Habits. The secret is not a magic potion or insight or innate driving force that some have and others do not. The secret is simply to **do whatever it takes to establish positive habits.** You have probably heard of positive and negative spirals. When things are going well in one area, you reap benefits in others. For example, if you look after your health and exercise regularly, you benefit in a number of ways. You typically will eat healthier, knowing that you have a workout coming up; your clothes will fit better, so you will feel less stress; you will look at the world in a more positive and optimistic manner; and so on. The simple act of sticking to a solid exercise plan pulls you into an upward spiral where the implications go far beyond the exercise itself.

The same thing happens in reverse with downward spirals. Say, for example, you are not able to exercise because of a bad injury. The lack of exercise makes you feel worse and look at the world in a more pessimistic light. You start eating more junk food because you get bored, and the downward spiral continues. Trying to be on an upward spiral as much as possible is a worthy goal to have. **The secret is simply to replace bad habits with good ones.**

There are many books out there that discuss how to build positive habits, and the one I would draw your attention to is *Atomic Habits,* by James Clear. This book is one of the most practical ones you can find on how to think about habits and how to build the right ones for yourself.* In particular I want to emphasize to you the idea of attaching new habits to existing ones. For example, I found it very easy to start new (and give up old) habits when moving houses, since I was already going through such a big change anyway.

For example, the real value of a personal trainer is not the motivational techniques and the "rah rah rah" support that they provide. That positive enthusiasm makes up only about half of the value. The main advantage is establishing a routine of exercise that pushes you past the initial difficult stages. I have found that establishing a habit typically takes about twenty days. If you can

* As an aside, there are many books out there that provide you with knowledge. But knowledge isn't really the issue when you are trying to achieve something great. What really counts is the ability to get things done. It is not about knowing but about doing that is critical. *Atomic Habits* goes into great detail on *how* to do things, and that is why I think it is an essential addition to your library.

maintain a habit every day for twenty days, it will typically sink in and you will not have to try much harder to continue. Those twenty days are key, and you should do whatever you can to not break the streak until you've built the habit.

The quality of ambivalence is great to have while interpreting situations and maintaining balance, and it's something you should cultivate. There are many things in life that you cannot control. For example, if you are travelling to a meeting, there are many possible things that may derail your timing. One of the secrets to a stress-free life is to try to remain ambivalent to outcomes. This does not mean that you don't care, but simply that you will be OK with any outcome.

We must accept that some things are in your control, such as the discipline to get up every morning, and some are out of your control, such as the weather. The key is **reframing things to be in your control** (e.g., don't think that you are afraid of heights; instead, say that you are afraid of falling). So you can focus on how to reduce your fear by, for example, training in mountain climbing.

Never stop pushing to get to further heights. Remember, people do not grow old. When they stop growing, they become old. Do something that you love to do every day. Try to get multiple perspectives by spending time with people over the age of seventy and under the age of six. Their experiences, approaches to life, and interpretations of situations will prove refreshing and help keep you grounded.

Finally, it is worth framing in your mind the ability to **move on from situations and to let go**. Ninety percent of what you worry about never happens. Of the other 10 percent that does happen, most things are never as bad as what you imagined. So relax! Worrying is similar to sitting on a rocking chair—it keeps you occupied but ultimately gets you absolutely nowhere. Think what you need to about a situation, and then let it go.

Small things, such as road rage, bother small minds. Most small things are simply not worth your time or energy to worry about. **Try to always tell the truth**. If you lie, then part of your brain becomes occupied with remembering that lie, and you therefore cannot use your whole brain for any subsequent task. Truth also usually simplifies a situation, is inescapable and eternal, and will allow you to grow and mature. A proverb to finish the chapter that reminds us of the importance of doing for others:

> *If you want happiness for an hour—take a nap.*
> *If you want happiness for a day—go fishing.*
> *If you want happiness for a year—inherit a fortune.*
> *If you want happiness for a lifetime—*
> *help someone else.*
>
> **—CHINESE PROVERB**

SUMMARY AND KEY LEARNING POINTS

- Getting and remaining healthy is crucial to your well-being and happiness. No matter what you achieve, if you don't have good health to enjoy it with, it will not satisfy you in the optimal way.

- Listen to your body and try different food and drink combinations to feel what works. It is hard to just accept various experts' views, so get into the habit of trial and error.
- Being healthy is much more than just a personal goal. It is one of the greatest gifts you can give to others around you, as you can be fully present for them.
- Have as much natural food and drink as you can, and try to avoid processed foods.
- Detoxify yourself regularly. Toxins will accumulate in your body, and you need to flush them out to maintain proper health.
- Watch out for marketing ploys to get you to eat poorly purely for the profit of the producers.
- Drink as close to eight to thirteen glasses of water (depending on your size) every day, and start each morning with one big glass of water.
- Limit your intake of the three whites: flour, sugar, and salt.
- Make it an aim to stay as positive as you can, and try to avoid getting angry. Worrying constantly is also usually pointless and damaging.
- Try to limit the medicine you take to what is absolutely necessary.
- Exercise as much as you can, and take up activities that you can commit to keep doing. Walking is a wonderful way to connect with nature and to help dissipate stress.
- Life is about deciding which priorities to focus on and when. You cannot be going full speed on all

aspects of your life at one time (such as relationships, family, career/study, and so on). Choose how you spend your time wisely, and appreciate that you can achieve balance, but only in the long run.

- Meditation is fantastic if you can do it, but consider repeating affirmations as an alternative way to achieve that peace of mind.
- Life can be like a pressure cooker. You need vents.
- Habits are the secrets to staying motivated and getting to your goals. Replace bad habits with good ones to see real progress.
- Do something that you love to do every day.
- Try to get multiple perspectives by spending time with people over the age of seventy and under the age of six. Their differing views and priorities will help enlighten your mind with what is possible.
- Try to remain as ambivalent as possible to outcomes, especially those that you cannot control. It all happens for a reason.

Exercises

FOOD / DRINK AWARENESS

When it comes to your diet, the way to kickstart health is to firstly become aware of what exactly you put into your body. Over the next week, keep a journal of everything that you eat and drink. In particular, pay attention to the following table:

HEALTHY **Want to have more of**	**UNHEALTHY** **Want to have less of**
Water	Alcohol and sugary drinks
Fruit	Added sugar
Vegetables	Added salt
Nuts and seeds such as almonds, Brazil nuts, chia seeds, and flaxseed	Flour foods such as white bread, pastries, cookies, cakes, and muffins
Fish	Pizza
White meat (although not too much)	Red meat
Beans and legumes	Fast food
Eggs (limit to no more than one per day)	Chips

Once you have a week's worth of entries in your journal, you will have a great starting point to make some decisions on where you need to adjust your diet. Remember, it is a marathon and not a sprint, so it's fine to make changes slowly over time. If you rush and try to do too much at the same time, the chances of falling off your health kick increase considerably. Remove one or two unhealthy foods and drinks per week, and add one or two healthy foods and drinks per week. The changes will add up, and your goal is to feel completely different in six months rather than just one week.

Also note: Nutrition is a highly controversial subject. I have developed these lists of what you should and shouldn't have purely from my own experience of what makes me feel good, and what does the opposite. Many of the unhealthy foods and drinks are well marketed and may make you feel good in the short term by satisfying cravings. Anything in moderation may be OK for you, but you must listen to your body (and your doctor) and aim to have a healthy long-term body that will support you as you age.

AFFIRMATIONS

Affirmations have helped me tremendously in life to provide focus, train my mind, and keep hope for what I want to achieve. Nearly every single one of my affirmations has come true, and I encourage you to take a little time to develop your own affirmations. There are many resources that can help you, and the exercise below provides the basic points.

- First, write down what you really want in life. You may wish to reference the core values you developed in the Love and Relationships chapter. You can also consider what you want for different domains of your life, such as money, career, learning, and so on.
- Translate what you want into sentences which:
    - Start with "I am ..."
    - Use the present tense whenever possible, that is, as if you are already exhibiting the desired behaviour.

- Make them as concise as possible, because you will be repeating them often. Each of my affirmations are twelve to fifteen words long, on average.
- For focus, try to narrow down your list of affirmations to six or seven. Make sure your final affirmation is one of gratitude, namely, "Thank you for ..."

Once you have your affirmations, try to repeat them as often as possible during the day. You may need to have them written initially, but soon you will commit them to memory through repetition. Some people like saying them when they are in the shower. Others will repeat them when they are driving or walking. You do not want to get to the obsessive stage, but try to repeat them as often as is reasonable. It is best to make repeating them a habit, and for that I would suggest attaching them to something you do every day. For me, that is walking, and I will explain in our next exercise.

WALKING

Now that you have affirmations, you can pair them with another exceedingly healthy practice: walking.

- Go for as long a walk as you can, splitting it up into two parts.
- Spend the first half repeating your affirmations in your head. Take them one at a time, and repeat each one for at least five to ten minutes. When you feel your mind start wandering into other thoughts, gently bring it back to your affirmations.
- Try to breathe through your nose as much as possible.

- Let your mind wander and enjoy the second half of the walk.
- Repeat the walk as often as you can, and at least three to four times per week.

REFLECTION QUESTIONS

- Does your diet help you achieve optimal health? If not, what habits must you drop and/or develop to get to that optimal health?
- How do you feel when you have no reason to feel anything? Obviously, you will feel good if you come across some good news or are anticipating something positive, and you will feel bad if you receive some bad news or punish your body in some way. But on a scale of 1 to 10 for energy, how do you feel first thing in the morning, or when you have no reason to feel good or bad at all? When you wake up, do you feel closer to a 10 (where you are almost bouncing off the walls and are ready to take on the world), or closer to a 1 (where you feel so tired you just want to go back to bed)? Is this how you want to feel? If not, what can you do to feel better?
- Do you get enough sleep? How about too much sleep? What effect does this have on you, your energy levels, your interactions with others, etc.?
- When was the last time you felt at peace with yourself and the world around you?
- What habits do you maintain (positive and negative)?

CHAPTER 5

LEARNING

"Perfection is not attainable, but if we chase perfection we can catch excellence."

—VINCE LOMBARDI

As an individual, you should always be looking to grow. If you are standing still, then you are actually moving backwards. Why? Because the whole world and everyone else in it is moving forwards. This holds true not only for individuals but also for organizations. We have examined how to get your body healthy, and we will now concentrate on the mind. **Learning new things is the best way to keep yourself young and your brain sharp**. Education is what sets us free. Most people spend a fortune on feeding their bodies but a relatively minute amount on feeding their minds. The only time you are actually growing is when you are a little uncomfortable.

Why will learning new things contribute to your happiness? Let's think for a moment as to how you can make yourself happy. You can choose to focus in two broad areas:

- **Pleasures**—For example, indulging in your favorite food, watching a great movie, going on holiday, and so on.
- **Gratifications**—For example, learning a new hobby, learning a language, volunteering for something that you believe in and support, and so on.

Basically, the difference is that for gratifications you have to use some energy and time, you have to actually try. Pleasures are typically immediate and simple to indulge in, but gratifications require you to make a significant effort and will delay the feeling of success or reward. People who spend more time investing in delayed gratification instead of instant pleasures are infinitely happier on every level, and incidentally, they are way more successful than those who concentrate on just pleasures.

This helps explain why there are billionaires who can do whatever they want but are not happy. They indulge in pleasures too much and forget about gratifications. Similarly, some of the happiest people I know have very little in terms of material possessions but feel they are making a difference in the world around them by investing in delayed gratifications. Consider where you spend your time and how you try to make yourself happy. We will return to pleasures and gratifications later on in this chapter.

Remember, **you do not have to learn only from your *own* mistakes**. Empathetic people will learn from other people's mistakes, too, and the more empathetic you are, the easier it is to do so. Try putting yourself in other people's shoes and learning from what they go through. If you just learn through making your own mistakes, your scope is limited, because your life is limited in time. Learn from others, and you will end up learning a whole lot more overall. Going even further, a wise man can learn from others' mistakes, whereas a fool cannot even learn from his own mistakes. You learn from others when you are nonjudgemental. The lack of judgement helps you read a situation clearly and in an unbiased manner, and therefore makes the situation perfect to learn from.

We will start this chapter with one of the best ways to expand your horizons—by getting up and travelling.

PACK YOUR BAG

> *"Travel is more than the seeing of sights; it is a change that goes on, deep and permanent, in the ideas of living."*
>
> **—MIRIAM BEARD**

As I remind all of my students, you learn more travelling than you do in any classroom (hard for me to say as a teacher, but true!). In fact, if you are ever feeling a little lost about life and your place in it, just go and travel. Things will invariably seem different, and often better, when you have another perspective and you are able to get away from it all.

I believe that during the COVID-19 pandemic, we suffered in many ways due to the unexpected nature of the disease and the unpredictability of what lay ahead. My son was very young at the time, and his generation went through several years where they could not mix and mingle as they normally would. This affected their development in social situations. Many people died or became seriously ill, and the tragedies that we heard of on a daily basis turned the world upside down for many years. One of the key consequences of COVID-19 for those who did not get seriously ill was the loss of being able to travel freely. I believe this had a huge influence on our psyche, and for anyone who enjoys travel, it was awfully frustrating.

We live in a time now where we are lucky enough to be able to visit almost all areas of the world. Our passports (and some funds) help us travel to places far and wide, allowing us to witness the most amazing parts of our planet. Never before have we been so connected. You could visit many completely new places every year of your life and not even get close to seeing all there is to see. **Taking in the sights, smells, and sounds of different places educates the mind and provides perspective.** Try to travel as much as you can, and take advantage of being able to see so much more of the world than our previous generations could.

It was a brisk morning in May when my wife and I decided to go for a hike up the Stawamus Chief. The "Chief," as it is known locally, is one of the largest granite monoliths in the world; it towers over seven hundred meters (2,297 feet) above the waters of Howe Sound and is adjacent to the town of Squamish in British Columbia. My wife grew up with a front-row view of the Chief, so it holds a special place in her heart. The Chief has three impressive summits, and we were heading to the Second Peak (or the Centre Summit) for our hike. Near the top, some places are so rugged and tricky, there are short sections where chains and ladders have been bolted to the rock for aid.

When we got near the top, there was a particularly challenging section where the ground was slippery and steep, and we wondered if we could even make it to our goal. We paused for a while, and then we saw a hiker returning from the top, almost running towards us. It seemed that he had not only reached the top with ease but was running down to go and scale one of the other peaks. He encouraged us by saying, "You're nearly there!"

I mumbled in return (I was *very* tired and a little disheartened by being so close yet feeling so far) something along the lines of, "This ain't easy."

His reply struck a chord in my heart and has remained with me since: "Nothing worthwhile ever is." What a fantastic way of looking at things, especially when you are struggling.

Why are people generally ruder in big cities? I think it is down to the lack of physical space and crowdedness. People need space, and if they cannot get it physically, then they put up an invisible mental barrier to stop others from intruding on their personal space. The abundance of strange people also stifles the desire for interaction. One of the reasons I love Vancouver and British Columbia is the feeling I get when returning home. Previously, I only lived in big cities around the world, and there was a mixed feeling when returning from vacation or a work trip. I would be happy to be returning home but sad to see all of the pollution and congestion. And I often had a slight sinking feeling knowing that I would have to get back into my usual work habits. However, when returning to Vancouver, it does not matter if I have had the very best holiday or trip. I see the mountains and the water, and I experience a feeling of deep joy and gratitude to be able to call this place home.

Another big difference (which helps explain why I love where I live) between where I used to live (Europe) and where I live now (British Columbia) is the feeling present when travelling almost anywhere locally. In Europe, wherever you stand, it is marvelous to consider that, before your time, literally thousands of people have stood in exactly the same spot. In British Columbia, you can take a few steps off the beaten path and stand in a spot where literally no one has ever been! When my son was younger, my favorite game to help him fall asleep while I was driving was to have him count the trees that we pass. It helped him sleep and reminded me of the fabulous nature all around us.

If you are able to travel for work, try to make sure that you have some free time just before you leave or after you arrive so that you can stay and enjoy the region/city. Or even better, so that you can go somewhere close by to explore further. Become a tourist for a day in your hometown, seeing the sights and finding out things you never knew. We often never get around to seeing all of the gems on our doorstep because we feel they are so close and we can see them any time. Indeed, I have often unearthed great local places previously not experienced by myself when showing around people from out of town, simply because we are now acting like tourists do. Remember, the shortest way to get anywhere is to have company travelling with you. There is so much around you that you simply just have to tune into. You could walk down the same street one hundred times and notice a different thing every time. It is all there waiting for you—you just need to make the time and space in your own mind to receive it.

As a final note on travelling, consider the following quote by Mark Twain:

"Twenty years from now you will be more disappointed by the things that you didn't do than by the ones you did do. So throw off the bowlines. Sail away from safe harbor. Catch the trade winds in your sails. Explore. Dream. Discover."

CURIOSITY

> *"He who asks a question remains a fool for five minutes. He who does not ask remains a fool forever."*
>
> **—CHINESE PROVERB**

When was the last time you did something for the first time? If you wish to get into the habit of lifelong learning, then you must develop a sense of curiosity. Why is the world the way it is? How did cities and civilizations develop? Why is there so much inequality in the world? Why do some always seem to thrive and some always seem to struggle? None of these questions are simple to answer, but thinking about them and cultivating a mindset to explore and satisfy your curiosity is a sure way to make the most of your life. How do you know what is possible if you haven't surveyed the entire landscape? Heightening your wisdom to make the most out of all situations is a primary goal of this book.

Don't be afraid to ask dumb questions. They are easier to handle than dumb mistakes. As Albert Einstein reminded us, "Imagination is more important than knowledge." Try new things and experiment. When you are looking for what sparks your interest, fewer commitments and more experiments make sense. When you discover what lights your fire, then fewer experiments and more commitments will drive you forward. To achieve the impossible, one must think outside of the box, to look where everyone else has looked but see what no one else has seen. This ability to think outside of the box is critical to becoming an effective leader, and indeed helps separate us from Artificial Intelligence (as of the time of writing).

Procrastination is one of the greatest enemies of curiosity. When you are curious about something, you need to follow up that curiosity quickly by looking into further information or talking to others about it. If you see an interesting advertisement on your way home, make sure you look it up quickly or talk to someone about it as soon as you can. This will prevent procrastination taking hold of you and causing you to forget what you even found interesting in the first place. **A creative mess is far better than idle neatness.** While we are on the topic, try to let procrastination work for you. We all procrastinate from time to time. The longer you leave something undone, the harder it is to get it started. Therefore, when you are tempted to do something you know you *shouldn't* do, just pause and wait for a while. Procrastination may just ensure that you never get to it!

Higher-quality questions are crucial to your way of being. **People who achieve a lot typically ask better-quality questions.** For example, let's say you are trying to figure out a workout routine. If you simply ask yourself, "How can I work out?" then you will likely get a quality of answer commensurate with the simplicity of the question. That is, not a great answer. If you expand the question to "How can I work out doing something that I enjoy?" you will get a little closer to a reasonable answer. If you go further and ask, "How can I work out doing something that I enjoy and that

I can easily sustain every week?" then you might get somewhere. We typically use our minds very well to react to challenges, but we don't use them enough to be proactive and build a better life. Get into the habit of asking better-quality questions. The more intelligent the question, the more valuable the answer is likely to be.

Moving to the other side of the equation, no matter the scope of the question, you will find that **the *best* answer is often the most *direct* one**. For example, to answer the question of how to avoid paying speeding tickets, you could do any combination of the following. You could spend lots of time figuring out how not to get caught (for example, bypassing speed cameras, figuring out locations of speed traps, figuring out how to annul speeding tickets, and so on). Or instead, you can just follow the simple two words: Don't speed. You will be guaranteed to never get a ticket.

When you are curious, you learn to listen more. Listening is a key skill that will help you in communication, relationships, and understanding. **We are typically not very good listeners**. We are born with two eyes, two ears, but one mouth for a very good reason. The mouth can be a piercing weapon that can cause untold harm to those around you. Remember, try to **talk less and listen and see more** to understand what is happening around you. Personally, I find this difficult, as I very much like to talk. When I look back, though, some of my deepest insights have come when I simply stop and listen to what is around me (either people or places).

Why are we so poor at listening? What do you normally do when you are supposed to be listening? Most people are actually thinking of what they want to say next and are just waiting for a convenient pause in the other person's speech so they can jump in. You can see this clearly when someone comes to you on a Monday morning and asks how your weekend was. Before you have even finished your first sentence, they jump in and start telling you about their weekend. They had no intention to really learn about your weekend but thought it would be rude to just start talking about their weekend. So instead, they asked you about your weekend first, but their early jumping in reveals what they really wanted to do.

I have been fascinated by effective listeners, and more specifically, by how some people seem to have what we call magnetic personalities, for many years. There are some folks who, after you spend a little time with them, you wonder where they have been all of your life! They seem to really understand you and get what you are trying to say, as if you have known each other forever. I have always wondered, *How do they do it?* Do they have some innate quality or skill? Have they been gifted some form of irresistible personality that others cannot refuse? After observing many such interactions, I can break it down to my four levels of listening.

PERRY'S 4 LEVELS OF LISTENING

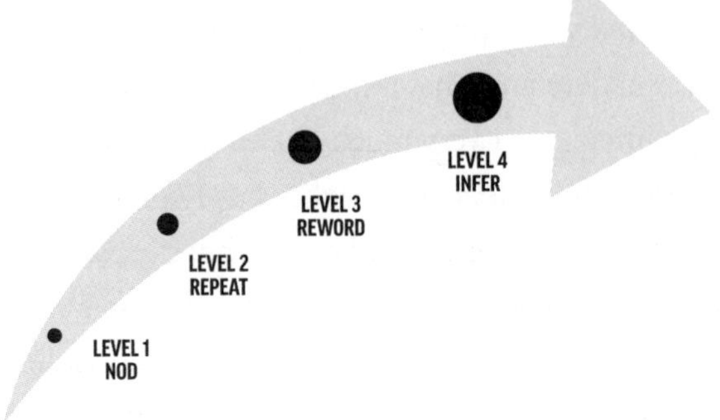

Allow me to explain the different levels of listening with an example. Let's say you walk into work in the morning when it is particularly damp outside, and you take off your jacket, proclaiming, "It's pouring rain outside!" If all I do is look into your direction and nod, then I am a Level 1 listener. Note, I may not have even heard exactly what you said—I just know that you mumbled a few words in my direction, and I acknowledged you. This is the most basic level of listening.

A Level 2 listener will repeat back to you what you just said. So in our example, I would respond to you with something like, "Oh, is it pouring rain outside?" Why is this better than a Level 1 listener? Well, now I have proven to you that I actually *heard* everything you said. At Level 1, I simply acknowledged that you said something, but I may not have even heard the precise words.

A Level 3 listener will go further and *reword* what you have just said. In our example, that might mean me responding with "Oh, is it raining heavily outside?" I have simply reworded what you said to me. This is better than a Level 2 listener, because I have demonstrated to you that I *understood* what you said. I cannot reword if I do not understand the initial words.

A Level 4 listener will go even further and try to infer some *meaning* from what you have just said. After all, communication is trying to get across to others what is going on in your own head. In our example, I may respond to your initial comment by jumping ahead and stating, "You are probably not going to be in the best mood for our first meeting today." I heard you, I understood you, and now I have tried to ascertain some meaning from your words. Note, I may be wrong. You may love walking out in the rain! Level 4 listeners are usually excellent at adjusting what they say, and their empathy allows them to get it wrong some times.

Why do the four levels of listening work so well for learning? In a typical conversation, you say something, and then I say something, and you say something, etc., and we gradually get deeper. With Level 4 listeners, the jumping ahead and inferences mean that you get very deep, very quickly. At the end of this chapter, there is an exercise to become a Level 4 listener. Try it and see what happens. Why are we not all already at a Level 4? Simple, it can be exhausting if you are not used to it. Try to really tune in to what someone is saying and infer some meaning. You will find it can tire you out, especially if you have never really consciously tried previously.

To learn effectively, we have to take in information accurately. If you want to help people, you must understand what is going wrong for them. If you don't truly listen to someone, how can you properly help them? This is similar to trying to work a complex piece of machinery having only read a small fraction of the user manual. **If you want to make the world a better place, you must accurately understand what is happening right now and how it is affecting people**. And you do that by listening. Listening to people and taking an active interest in what they are saying not only deepens your understanding but also shows the other person that you care and that they matter. Making others feel this way makes it even more likely they will open themselves up further.

HOW TO LEARN

Get into the habit of experimenting and trying things out first. It's OK to make mistakes. **If you are not making any mistakes, you probably are not working on difficult enough issues,**

and that in itself could be a huge mistake. The definition of insanity is doing the same thing over and over and expecting different results. Try something new. A good analogy is to think of your mind as a parachute. It only functions when it is open. Albert Einstein got it spot-on when he stated, “The significant problems we have cannot be solved at the same level of thinking with which we created them.”

Children learn best when they can try for themselves, rather than by us holding their hands through all situations. A lifetime spent making mistakes is better than a lifetime doing nothing. **Make sure you try first before asking others for help**. Not only will you likely learn more and faster, but others will be far more willing to help you if they know that you have tried some alternatives and have used initiative instead of simply (and perhaps lazily) seeking help straight away.

If you came to me and said, “I don’t understand how XYZ works. Can you help me?” I may choose to help, or I may not. However, if you came to me and said, “I don’t understand how XYZ works. I have tried to look at the following sources and have spoken to the following people, and I thought it was ABC. But the more I think about it, it could also be DEF or RST depending on the situation. Can you help me?” I am far more likely to want to help because I can see that you have already made a reasonable attempt to figure it out yourself.

Children don’t lack capacity; they just lack teachers.

> *“All children are born geniuses; 9,999 out of every 10,000 are swiftly, inadvertently degeniusized by grownups.”*
>
> **—BUCKMINSTER FULLER**

STRIVE FOR EXCELLENCE

> *"Mastery is the best goal because the rich can't buy it, the impatient can't rush it, the privileged can't inherit it, and nobody can steal it. You can only earn it through hard work. Mastery is the ultimate status."*
>
> **—DEREK SIVERS, *HOW TO LIVE: 27 CONFLICTING ANSWERS AND ONE WEIRD QUESTION***

Learning is essential when you wish to strive for maximum success, because it helps you get better through continuous improvement, adaptation to any kind of change, and the development of further skills and knowledge needed to thrive in future environments. Keen learners are constantly looking for ways, large and small, to improve. Just getting better by 1 percent per day will lead to enormous results in time. **Learning leads you to have a growth and abundance mindset, which helps identify new possibilities and overcome challenges to achieving your full potential.**

Whatever you choose to go into, make sure you do so with all of your energy. Do not give it a half-hearted go; instead, launch into things with the vigor of someone who is on a mission. You may not get to the very top, but your striving for excellence will separate you from the crowd and ensure you feel fulfilled and content with your results because of all the effort you put in. **Success is not always guaranteed, but failure is certain if you don't even try in the first place.** The problem in life is not that people aim too high and miss it, but that they aim too low and hit it. Failure defeats losers, but actually does the opposite and inspires leaders.

Stay away from the naysayers who preach maxims such as (a slightly tongue-in-cheek) "If practice makes perfect, and nobody's perfect, then why practice?" You don't practice to become perfect. It's not the result that matters as much as the journey to get there. If you are learning to drive, then the driving license (the result if successful) is not the most important part. If it was, then just getting a license would mean everything. No, it is instead the skills and behaviours you learned to help get the license that really matter. These skills and behaviours are going to make the difference in your future driving, and not the physical license itself. Most of the time, the real difference is made by how you frame a situation. As Henry Ford reminded us, "Whether you think you can or you think you can't, you're right." What an empowering way to look at the world!

Remember to take off the hand brakes! Do you ever feel that no matter how hard you try, you're not getting anywhere? Do you feel that you're doing everything right and giving it your all, but nothing is happening? Maybe you need to identify the metaphoric handbrakes in your life that are stopping you. It may be painful, as they often come from the people closest to you or from things that you have always strongly assumed to be true, but deep introspection may reveal otherwise. Ask the intelligent question: Is what I'm doing helping me move towards worthy goals or not?

To get smarter, you must play against smarter people. If you are the smartest person in the room, you are in the wrong room! When you mix with smarter people, their ideas rub off on you and they open your mind to previously unexplored avenues. Simply comparing your thoughts and ideas on any topic to those whom you respect and believe to be smarter will cause you to learn for the future. What do you normally talk about when you're with friends? Do you gossip a lot? Do you cast judgement on others? Do you feel better when you put others down or make fun of them? You may feel temporarily better when doing any of the above, but they are extremely destructive practices to your soul. Eleanor Roosevelt put it best when she said:

"Great minds discuss ideas; average minds discuss events; small minds discuss people."

You want to lead by example. Don't expect others to listen to your advice and ignore your example. It is easy to say the right words, but it's really your actions that will be most observed and internalized. Children learn this early in terms of replicating the behaviour of their parents, rather than simply doing what they are told to do. Giving advice is infinitely easier than following it, but when you follow it, others will follow you.

Persistence, patience, and discipline are important when you strive for excellence. When you keep practicing and keep trying, any task will become easier. Note, it is not that the task has become simpler; it is exactly the same as it always was. You have become stronger. Aristotle got it right many years ago when he said: "We are what we repeatedly do. Excellence then is not an attribute, but a habit."

EDUCATION AND INTELLIGENCE

> *"You may leave school, but it never leaves you."*
>
> —**ANDY PARTRIDGE**

Knowledge is not power, but *potential* power. It has to be organized and directed for it to become useful. Knowledge properly *applied* is power.

Life is like a school, and you are here to learn. Problems are simply part of the curriculum that appear and fade away like an algebra class, but the lessons you learn will last a lifetime. Having worked in higher education for over twenty years, I have seen some very clear patterns in those who succeed in any field, and one of their key characteristics is to commit to lifelong learning. They appreciate that they do not know everything, and there is so much to learn. Sure, generations change, and we cannot keep teaching people like we did in the past. In my experience, the younger generations are way more tech savvy and suffer a little in terms of constant distractions. However, as teachers, we need to embrace these changes and figure out ways to reach and inspire subsequent generations. After all, they will be looking after us when we grow old!

How do you know if you are behaving intelligently? **Acting intelligently is doing anything that moves you towards your goals**. Acting unintelligently is doing anything that moves you away from your goals. Of course, you need to have worthy goals to start off with, and once you do, it will make this framework a lot easier to abide by. (There is a goal-setting exercise in the Conclusion.)

Intelligence is a way of acting and not necessarily just your

IQ. It is all about moving towards your goals and doing positive things. If you do things in a negative manner, or do something that moves you away from your goals, hurts someone, or is against your morals and values, then you are acting stupidly or unintelligently, regardless of how high your IQ is. There are countless examples of very smart people doing very silly things. As Mark Twain so eloquently puts it: "The problem with common sense is that it is not too common!"

Stupidity is relatively harmless, but intelligent stupidity is highly dangerous. When you have the knowledge and skills to make a difference, use them to make a *positive* difference. **Help people, move ideas forward, and try not to harm anyone with your new power.** Making progress does not always mean getting more. It's not always a good thing to keep *adding* things to your life. Sometimes you make the most progress by figuring out what to *take away*.

When I think of the very best doctors, they are not the ones who blind me with all of the technical terms and possibilities for my ailments. Rather, the very best ones remove all of the noise and narrow things down to what their expertise tells them. These doctors come across as wise because they focus on what will really help me rather than focusing on proving their proficiency. The very best specialists I have dealt with will ask a few pointed questions and then conclude by telling me, "Out of everything it could be, I believe it is XYZ, and this is what you should do about it." The worst specialists will cite almost encyclopedic definitions of what my condition could be, proving that they know what they are supposed to, but not actually helping me at all. I could have googled all that myself. A true expert marries the knowledge with their experience and ends up helping you.

Invest as much as you can in getting a good education. It is never too late to learn new things, and we regularly see older students taking university and college classes to try to improve or simply learn. **The education is in itself an investment towards your future**. Derek Bok (former President of Harvard University) put it nicely when he said, "If you think education is expensive, try ignorance."

When considering the future, keep in mind the following two quotes:

> *"Life can only be understood backwards; but it must be lived forwards."*
>
> **—SØREN KIERKEGAARD**

> *"You can't connect the dots looking forward; you can only connect them looking backwards. So you have to trust that the dots will somehow connect in your future."*
>
> **—STEVE JOBS**

When I think of life, I consider it to be one large jigsaw puzzle for each of us. Every year, a few more pieces go into your puzzle through your experiences and decisions. When you advance in years, you start to see the overall pattern and deepen your understanding as to why things have happened in your life. Why did you meet various people at different stages? Why did you go through so many ups and downs? What was the purpose of your key experiences? All of this becomes clearer as you age because the jigsaw puzzle becomes more complete (and you also are able to see what happens in other people's puzzles for perspective).

Have you ever been so focused on a part of a puzzle, that you didn't see the forest for the trees (that is, you were not able to make out the big picture because of all the detail)? Then one day, you took a step backwards, saw how that part of the puzzle connected to the rest, and breathed a sigh of satisfaction. That is exactly how you will feel when the puzzle pieces of your life come together. **You need to do all you can on a daily basis, but have faith that your puzzle is being built exactly the way it should be**. Try not to think too much about the future because you will become anxious and overwork your mind. A wise man is a master of his mind; a foolish man is a slave to his.

Being a teacher myself, I can tell you that the best way to learn something is to try and teach it to someone else. At Google, it is estimated around 55 percent of their courses are taught by current employees. Not only does this foster a culture of learning (and save Google a ton of money by not having to hire external consultants), but it also makes the employees who teach even more knowledgeable and expert in their respective fields. If you simply listen to information or read about something, you have little chance of recalling it a few weeks later. If you participate in a demonstration or see the information from a multitude of angles, you will recall a little more. If you try and teach it to someone, then your recall goes through the roof, because to teach it you really need to understand it at a profound level. If you are studying for any exam, grab a friend who knows nothing about the topic and proudly exclaim to them, "I am going to teach you something new today!"

EXERCISE YOUR BRAIN

> *"Live as if you were to die tomorrow. Learn as if you were to live forever."*
>
> **—GANDHI**

Reading does for the mind what exercise does for the body. **Your brain is like a muscle and needs to be worked.** Reading is very, very important, and you need to read a lot to understand a lot. You can find books, articles, and research on almost any topic, and your curiosity should lead you to explore whatever you are interested in. Pick any subject, and you can likely quickly find out what the most accomplished and knowledgeable people who have ever lived say about that topic.

Looking at the topic of reading from another direction, those who *choose not to* read are no better off than those who *cannot* read. It pains me when I see students graduate from high school and then vow that they will never read a book again in their life. Our education system causes them to become somewhat allergic to reading, and the saddest thing is when they keep their promise! You can always find topics that will interest you and that you can delve further into. This concept follows on what we have already talked about in terms of curiosity.

Reading not only gives you access to almost any information, but it also helps build your vocabulary and your intelligence. Remember the importance of mastering your language. **Language is how you express your thoughts.** People who are successful not only have a large vocabulary but also know how to express it in numerous ways. Crosswords (and even better: *cryptic* crosswords) help do the same. Reading a book on how to complete cryptic crosswords (and then going on to do at least one a day) is one of the best ways to build your vocabulary. I notice that when I enter a relatively wealthy person's home, they tend to have a huge library. And when I enter a relatively poor person's home, the biggest TV they can afford is front and center. TV itself is not a bad thing and can clearly be highly entertaining. Like most things however, you should only enjoy it in moderation.*

Why is reading so much more effective than watching TV or movies? When you watch a show of any kind, nearly all of the thinking has been done for you. The director or producer has thought about all of the sights and sounds that you will experience, and you can mainly sit back, relax, and enjoy. This is fine if you want to just relax. When reading though, the sights and sounds (even if they are expertly described) will not come close to putting the authors exact intentions in your mind. Instead, your mind has to fill these gaps with your own imagination. In a sense, you are cocreating the story that you are reading. You can read at your own pace and really internalize the points most salient to you. Finally, reading is much more a gratification than a pleasure. A mind stretched by new ideas can never return to its original dimensions, and you grow as a person.

With all of the literature that keeps being developed, we find that knowledge increases exponentially, but wisdom is in short

---

* As an aside, when I was younger, many TV shows used to come on once a week, and there was great satisfaction in talking about a show during the week with friends along with anticipating the next episode. The *delayed gratification* added to the enjoyment. Nowadays, you can stream entire seasons into a "binge-watch," which I find less satisfying because there is no delayed gratification, but rather, an instant pleasure. The lack of reflection time for each episode also takes away from the depth of the show.

supply. Remember, **knowledge is simply possessing information and facts, whereas wisdom is the ability to *apply* that knowledge effectively**. Indeed, this is part of the rationale of why I wrote this book. Read as much as you can, and try to spot patterns, especially across time and generations and across topics and industries. The patterns will help you develop your own sense of wisdom and understanding. Patterns are repeated in nature for a reason, and I believe part of that reason is to help you grow and grasp what is important.

If you really appreciate the beauty of reading, you may get to the stage of trying to write for yourself. Writing is one of the only ways to outlive yourself. People still read books from hundreds or even thousands of years ago. The author's physical life ended long ago, but their mental life remains alive and meaningful even today. You can leave a legacy by writing on any topic, but make it more powerful by writing about what you love and care about. It will be effortless and deeper than you can possibly imagine, and you will grow enormously by taking on such an enormous endeavour.

SUMMARY AND KEY LEARNING POINTS

- You need to keep working on yourself to grow. If you don't, you will actually be moving backwards since everything and everyone else is moving forwards.
- Spend more time on gratifications than indulging in pleasures, as gratifications will help you feel more fulfilled and closer to long-term happiness.

- Be empathetic and learn from other people's mistakes so as to avoid having to learn only from your own.
- Travel broadens your horizons like nothing else and can help you grow in many ways, because it broadens your mind to what is possible and opens your world to so many alternative perspectives.
- Develop a curiosity for the world around you. Whenever you are curious about anything, follow it up immediately by finding out more or talking to others about the topic.
- Procrastination is one of your greatest enemies. Do things as soon as reasonably possible, and don't keep waiting for the perfect time.
- Try to get into the habit of asking better-quality questions and listening at a Level 4 to improve the accuracy of information being taken in.
- It's better to try something than to sit around thinking about it. Give it all your heart, as striving for excellence will deepen your learning.
- Acting intelligently is doing anything that moves you towards worthy goals. Acting unintelligently is doing anything that moves you away from worthy goals.
- Life is like one big jigsaw puzzle where a few more pieces go in every year. Stand back occasionally to examine your jigsaw puzzle, and keep the faith that it will all turn out exactly as it is supposed to.
- Reading is the best exercise for the mind. To learn a lot, you must read a lot.

Exercises

ASKING BETTER QUESTIONS IN SERVICE OF BETTER ANSWERS AND LEARNING

For some people, asking good questions comes easily. Their natural curiosity, ability to read a situation and others around them, and extensive vocabulary allow them to frame good questions quickly and intuitively. For the rest of us, though, we lack the practice and innate talent to pose better questions that will lead to more helpful answers.

The good news is that you can get better with practice. When asking people questions, you want to ask open-ended ones (those questions that cannot be answered with a simple "yes" or "no") to help the other person open up and go in whatever direction they feel like, and follow-up questions to probe deeper into a topic and therefore deepen your understanding.

For this exercise, we are going to practice asking *yourself* better questions to help your personal growth. These questions will typically be a little longer but will allow you to focus on and think about answers that are more targeted and helpful for your growth.

In the following table, think about what would be a better alternative question to the one provided:

SIMPLE QUESTION	BETTER ALTERNATIVE QUESTION
How can I exercise more?	How can I exercise more doing something I love and something that I can do at least four times every week?
How can I do better at school or work?	
How can I become a better [son/daughter/brother/sister/parent/colleague]?	
How can I become more efficient?	
How can I become a more active member of my community?	
How can I make the world a better place?	

Note, the simple questions can be useful because they are short, open-ended, and can foster creativity, but the longer alternative questions are more useful to provide targeted solutions to specific issues. Neither type of question is better or worse than the other, and getting used to both types will help you take a holistic approach. The simple open-ended questions can provide inspiration but can also be overwhelming.

For more information on asking better questions, refer to the excellent article in the *Harvard Business Review*: "The Surprising Power of Questions.*

LEVEL 4 LISTENING

Listening is critical for learning because it's the main way we take in information, understand new concepts, and build knowledge and skills for our future. Being a good listener is a skill that you can learn. Reread the section on being a Level 4 Listener, and try the following exercise on the next three people you meet:

- Allow the conversation to flow as naturally as you can.
- When the other person says something, consider responding using any of the four levels:
    - Level 1—Sometimes it is best to simply acknowledge the other person with a nod and say nothing.
    - Level 2—Repeat back to the other person what they have just said.

* Alison Wood Brooks and Leslie K. John, "The Surprising Power of Questions," *Harvard Business Review*, May–June 2018, https://hbr.org/2018/05/the-surprising-power-of-questions.

- Level 3—Reword what the other person has just said to provide clarity and confirmation.
- Level 4—Infer (carefully) some meaning from what the other person has just said by using your logic and the context. (Note, you have to be flexible here. If your inference is wrong, correct it immediately by saying something along the lines of, "I'm sorry, I think I misinterpreted here—what exactly did you mean?").

- Make sure you pause after you respond at one of the levels to allow the other person time to speak.

The purpose of this exercise is to make you aware of the different levels of listening and the effects they have on the person you are listening to. Most people never stop to think about how they come across in a conversation because they are too preoccupied with what they want to say. Does moving up the levels open up the conversation or give you more of a connection with the other party? Do you feel the conversation goes deeper or stays the same? With a bit of practice, the levels will come naturally to you and an awareness will be built towards which level is appropriate and when.

REFLECTION QUESTIONS

- When was the last time you did something for the first time?
- Where in the world have you been that taught you the most about yourself?
- Where in the world would you like to visit and why?
- What would you do if you knew you could not fail?
- Which part of your life's jigsaw puzzle is complete, and which part confuses you?
- What have you done in the last two days to move you *towards* worthy goals?
- What have you done in the last two days to move you *away* from worthy goals?
- Are the people you spend the most time with helping you achieve your goals?
- How can you do more for your community and for those you love most?

CHAPTER 6

MONEY AND BUSINESS

"He is **poor** *who is dissatisfied; he is* **rich** *who is contented with what he has, and he is* **richer** *who is generous with what he has."*

—JAMES ALLEN,
THE PATH TO PROSPERITY **[EMPHASIS MINE]**

Money is one of the most controversial subjects that you can come across. Money is essential to do many things in life that you want to do, but how much do you really need? What amount would you be happy with? A million dollars? Two? Ten? When does money become a problem?

Don't kid yourself about the importance of money. It is

extremely important. Only fools or lazy people use excuses about how other things are more important. Yes, love, family, and friends are more important, but that does not mean money is not important. It is similar to asking which is more important, your arms or legs? Well, how about they are *both* important? It is not an either/or type of question.

A common misquote of the Bible that I hear from people is "money is the root of all evil." That is not the actual quote. The Bible does not say "money is the root of all evil." It says, "The *love* of money is the root of all evil" (emphasis mine). If you make money your primary love and you pursue affluence to the exclusion of or at the expense of other values, then yes it can be evil. But money itself is not evil; it depends on how you look at it. Money is great if you use it well and don't abuse it.

HOW TO THINK ABOUT MONEY

> *"What's money? A man is a success if he gets up in the morning and goes to bed at night and in between does what he wants to do."*
>
> **—BOB DYLAN**

Money can be incredibly empowering but can also get you into trouble. For most people, the trouble stems simply from the desire to have more money because they assume it will make them happier. No more worrying about bills or how you will survive in the future; instead, you will be able to afford whatever you want whenever you want it. It's worth pausing for a moment and thinking about what you would actually do if you came into lots of money.

When I ask individuals what they would do with lots of money, the answers are usually similar. For obvious reasons you would start by paying off any debts so you can have financial freedom and release the burden of owing. You may decide to indulge in certain possessions (such as a new house or car or clothes), which will bring you temporary happiness. You may also decide to indulge in various activities, such as eating at fancy restaurants, flying first class, and staying at high-end hotels, but as we discussed in a previous chapter, these indulgences will bring you only short-term happiness. There is nothing wrong with that, but just appreciate it will only make you happy for a little while.

What else would you do? Some would ensure they get into shape (or stay in shape) so that their good health will allow them to enjoy the money long into the future. Some would give a portion of the money away to help those less fortunate and in need. Some would invest to build something for the future. My response to all of these options: Can you not do that (or part of that) already? Sure, you may not be able to afford a personal trainer or fancy gym equipment, but you can certainly exercise more for free.

You may not be able to give away or invest as much money as you would if you were very rich, but you can still start and experience the same feeling with a little money. There is an exercise included at the end of this chapter to help drive this point home, but suffice it to say many of the things we think we would do if we had more money are actually available to us *now*. Maybe they are not available to the same scale, but they are available just the same.

Why do we really want money? I think a big part of it is experiencing the **freedom that lots of money can bring you**. When buying anything, you will not have to look at the price; instead, you can get exactly what you want. When travelling or choosing experiences, you can choose whatever you want without worrying about the cost. If you stay in very nice hotels and travel first class, you don't have to worry about food or drink or eating or drinking at certain times, because it will always be readily available close by. A perfect example of this in action is how you can usually tell when someone is new to a free buffet or free food or drink because they end up filling their plate to overflowing and indulging like a kid in a candy store. Meanwhile, people who are wealthy know there is plenty to go around and therefore there is no rush to get your fill.

Wealth can give you a mindset of abundance. There is more than enough money to make everyone rich. Do not view it as a zero-sum game. Do not believe that by you getting rich, someone else has to suffer or become poor. We can all become rich, and more importantly, we can all feel rich. Some things are simply priceless. But be careful. Don't let money get in the way of other things. Yes, it is extremely important, but occasionally take a step back and make sure it isn't causing you to *lose* things that money cannot buy, such as relationships. On your death bed, no one (including you) will care about how much money you made, but rather, how much of a difference you made. **You can't take it with you**. You are born with nothing and will die with nothing. Everything you do in the middle is really just a bit of fun! It's not about *having* what you *want*, but instead, *wanting* what you *have*.

Oprah Winfrey nailed it when she said:

"If you look at what you have in life, you'll always have more. If you look at what you don't have in life, you'll never have enough."

There will always be people in life who have more than you. If you get a nice house, then you will mix in circles where people have even nicer houses. If you get a swimming pool in your backyard, then you will mingle with others who own beautiful boats. If you get a boat, then you will see someone who has a helicopter. If you buy a helicopter, then you will meet someone who owns a private jet. And so on and so on. The point is if you are always looking for more, then you will never be satisfied and always feel lacking. The late, great Bob Marley reminds us, "The day you stop racing is the day you win the race." I would much rather live rich than die rich.

Remember to consider **there are many types of wealth.** For example, the obvious source of wealth is financial, and that includes all of your money and possessions (we sometimes call this your *net worth*). There is also social wealth, which stems from your status in a hierarchy. We have physical wealth, which comes in the form of your health. We have time wealth, which comes from your freedom to choose what you do. We have emotional wealth, which comes from the strength of your relationships. We have spiritual wealth, which comes from your contentment with life and your purpose.

TYPES OF WEALTH

FINANCIAL
Money
and Possessions

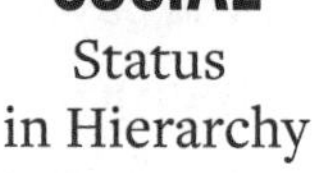

SOCIAL
Status
in Hierarchy

PHYSICAL
Health

TIME
Freedom to Choose

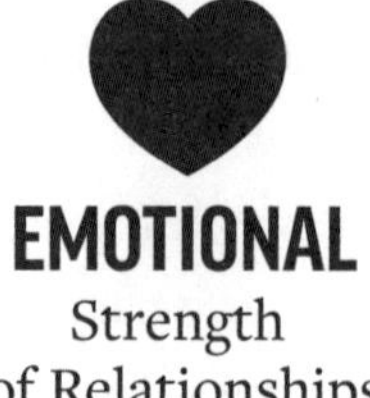

EMOTIONAL
Strength
of Relationships

SPIRITUAL
Contentment with
Life and Purpose

All of these types of wealth are linked. For example, if you obtain more financial wealth, you will likely be able to enjoy more time wealth. If you rise in social wealth, then you will also likely benefit in your financial wealth. However, there are times when these different types of wealth will conflict and compete with each other. For example, if you focus too much on financial wealth, you may lose your time and physical wealth. As with most things in this book, getting the balance right is key.

USING MONEY WISELY

> *"The measure of your life will not be in what you accumulate, but in what you give away."*
>
> **—DR. WAYNE DYER**

How can you make the most of the money that you have? A good rule of thumb is to split up the money you make into four buckets. Bucket 1 is for **spending** and includes all of your regular expenses, like housing, food, travel, etc. Bucket 2 is for **saving** and should be put in a safe place (such as a high-interest account in your bank). Bucket 3 is for **investing** and should be put towards items that could grow significantly in the future (such as real estate and stocks). Bucket 4 is for **giving,** for example, to charities and good causes. The proportions of these buckets may be different for everyone (and indeed will likely change as your financial status evolves), but they usually take on somewhere around the ratios of 70 percent spending, 10 percent saving, 10 percent investing, and 10 percent giving away. You can play around with these ratios and find one that suits your goals.

Over time, and as you hopefully earn more money, you will be able to dedicate more to the three buckets outside of spending. When you have a choice of which bucket to put extra money into, which should you choose? In my experience, you should put what you can into Bucket 4: giving away. From what I have seen, **the wealthiest people I know also give away the most money, and the more they give away, the more wealthy they seem to become**. The destinations of your giving should be determined by your values. What do you really care about? Who do you think deserves a share of your wealth? Indeed, focusing on your values helps determine where to spend your money as well. If, for example, you value learning, you may want to spend more on travel so that you can experience more cultures.

I cannot quite explain it, but money has a strange habit of making its way back to you (with interest) when you have used it wisely and given it to do something good. As Voltaire reminds us, "The man who leaves money to charity in his will is only giving away what no longer belongs to him." The time to give it away is while you are living and not just when you pass away. Givers have to set limits because takers rarely do.

Remember, the best things in life are free. Money can buy you an amazing house, but it cannot (directly) make a happy home. Money can get you the best medical professionals but cannot guarantee you good health. Money can buy you the best bed, but it does not guarantee you the best night of sleep. Looking at work, money can buy you a lofty position but cannot buy you respect. If you come into money, it often changes those around you more than it changes you. Be prepared for that, but don't let it drag you down, for you cannot control other people's perceptions. **You cannot control how other people behave or react, but you can decide to be humble and not show off.**

A few general tips to finish off this section:

- **Use credit cards only for convenience and never for credit.** Credit card providers make an astonishing amount of money simply because of the ridiculous interest rates they charge. Try your best to pay the debt on your card in full every month, and if you are unable to pay it all, then try to not use the credit card as much. Paying in full will also elevate your credit rating, which will be useful as your financial situation evolves.

- **Never buy something you don't need just because it is on sale.** It may be tempting, but it sets a dangerous precedent, and you don't want to waste money.

  There are some outlets that intentionally overprice initially just to offer things on sale, because they are tapping into your shortcut of the sale, affording you a good deal. This is much easier when you have financial goals or buckets that you are working your way towards, because they provide healthy decision objectives.

- **When lending people money, make sure their character exceeds their collateral.** You do not want to lose friends over money, but the right people will always make it a priority to pay you back as soon as possible. The wrong people will see the loan in a timeframe way longer than you can imagine. You cannot fundamentally change people, but you can choose to not go down the route of lending and trying to collect.

- **People who are wealthy will make money no matter what.** They will not make excuses, such as taxes or the government or the economy—they will thrive in all situations.

- As Warren Buffet put it: "Be fearful when others are greedy, and be greedy when others are fearful." **In other words, buy low and sell high!**

- **When buying something, look for quality and durability.** As Ben Franklin so eloquently put it: "The bitterness of poor quality remains long after the sweetness of low price is forgotten." I have found, for example, that you do not need to pay a fortune for designer clothes, but paying a little extra for higher-quality clothes (using better materials, offering more durability, etc.) goes a long way.

WORKING HARD

> *"Nothing will work unless you do."*
>
> **—MAYA ANGELOU**

"Plans are only good intentions unless they immediately degenerate into hard work."

—PETER DRUCKER

Working, and working hard with all of your heart, is crucial to your long-term happiness. You want to feel that you are making a difference and your toil is worth it. Not only will working hard give you the best chance of succeeding in whatever you do, but it will also satisfy you deeply to know that you have given something your all. Who do you think feels better (at a deep, spiritual level): the person who works hard and puts in a great shift every day, or the person who takes it easy and relaxes in a simple job? The person with the simple job may think they have hit the jackpot in doing something undemanding, but their soul is being destroyed by not even coming close to their full potential. It is not about making money but about making a difference. If you make enough of a difference, then the money will follow, no matter what you work in. **You will always have problems**. When you solve them, you get better-quality problems. That is the key, as you will get into the habit of forming better solutions.

Don't pursue money directly. Money is like happiness—it is an effect of the hard work that you put in. Pursue service and doing more, and money will take care of itself. Routine is the secret to getting things done. Look back at the Health and Well-Being chapter, where we discussed habits, to get ideas on how to build routines. I find it far easier to work out and stick to a good diet when I am working a lot. Why? Shouldn't it be easier during my holidays when, in theory, I have a lot more free time? No, it's actually harder precisely *because* I have more free time. The free time makes you somewhat lazier, and the (welcome) unpredictability and spontaneity when in this mode actually makes it harder to stick to a routine, which is what you need. Pretty ironic!

The journey is always more important than the destination. The greatest value is not in achieving your goals, but in who you become along the way. For example, if becoming a millionaire, the greatest value is not in the million dollars, but rather the skills, knowledge, discipline, and leadership qualities you'll develop in getting there. This helps explain why those who make their own money can lose it all and make it back quickly. They have learned all the skills to do it repeatedly. Conversely, lottery winners will often lose all of their money and be unable to get it back, because they never learned anything along the way and were simply lucky to get their winnings.

Always think about **adding value. Give people more than what they paid for, and give people more than what they ask for.** This is why having high levels of energy is critical for success. When you have lots of energy and someone asks you for three things, you won't give them three things, you will give them five. If, however, you are low on energy, you will barely be able to give them what they ask for. Those who exceed expectations are the ones who become the most successful. High energy also makes you more optimistic about life and is infectious, so it motivates those around you to make success even more likely.

Try to do what you really have a passion for. If you enjoy the work, time will fly. When you have a **career**, there are **not enough** hours in the day. When you don't like your job, there are **too many** hours in a day. This principle is the same for anything that we like or dislike. A movie, TV show, or book ends too quickly when we are really into it, but goes on forever if we are not enjoying it. A class or any kind of session where you are looking at your watch or the clock constantly is likely to be one that you do not enjoy.

(I distinctly remember playing games with time during my most boring MBA classes. I would intentionally not look at the clock for as long as possible, thinking the next time I do look at it, over one hour would have passed. To my horror, the time was never close to an hour but more like barely ten minutes!)

When working for others, consider the following two tips to help handle your boss and not get burned out.

First, in the situation of your boss asking you to do something when you are already at capacity. You have a clear dilemma here; namely, you don't want to let them down, but you also don't want to burden or overwhelm yourself further. What should you do? Simple: *Get them to make the choice.* Politely let them know all the things you have going on, and ask them nicely, "What would you like me to drop so that I can accommodate your request?" Your dilemma is only an issue if *you* make the decision, but if your boss makes the decision, all of the pressure is off.

Second, some advice on how to say no. I am very much a yes-man. I nod a lot when people talk to me, and in fact, I almost need a clamp to stop myself when I know I shouldn't be nodding so much (for example, in a negotiation). But again, I would feel bad if someone asked me for something, and I said no. So I ended up working later and later and sacrificing time with my family because I was getting home later and later.

The simple decision that changed my life was in how I framed the situation to myself. Previously, I would feel bad about saying no. But now, I look at it as a simple choice: Either spend time now helping someone and therefore need to stay later at work, or have an extra hour with my kids at home. When the decision was framed like that, I found it easy to say no, knowing that it was, in reality, saying yes to more time with my family.

On the theme of saying "no," consider the following two examples. Imagine you have just asked two colleagues for help in a particular situation.

One colleague replies, "Sorry, no, I cannot help you here."

The other colleague replies, "Thank you so much for asking me. I'm so sorry that I will not be able to help right now because I have too much to do today, but I would be happy to help in the future where possible, because I think you are doing something so very worthwhile."

Which one would you rather hear? Whom would you be more willing to help in the future? Learning to say no properly will help you stay firm and avoid situations that you do not want to be part of. It takes a little longer to get it right but is totally worth it in the long run.

FINDING WORK

If you are looking for a new position and wish to stick out at, say, a career fair, how do you do it? The problem is that you will be one of many (possibly hundreds of) folks who are trying to differentiate yourself and make a good impression on the potential recruiters. How do you ensure that they remember you? Once you have done a few of these fairs from the other side (i.e., as a recruiter), you will know exactly what to do.

I have hosted booths at fairs to recruit MBA students for my university in several parts of the world. I can tell you that I am asked the same ten or so questions multiple times in any session. "What is your university's competitive advantage?" "What is great about Vancouver?" "Who are your main competitors, and how do you compare to them?" and so on. If you ask any of these questions, I will not remember you at all. Why? Because I answer the same questions time and again and pretty much go on autopilot when answering.

The point is I am not really *thinking*. **You need to make me think**. How? Ask questions that make me stop and ponder. Something like, "What is the worst thing about your university?" or "What is the biggest mistake you make when recruiting students?" will certainly make me stop and think, because they are not the usual questions posed. You can make these questions a little more polished (see the exercise on asking better questions in the Learning chapter). But if you make me stop and think, you will break my record, and I will likely remember you at the end of the day, because my attention was high when we interacted.

Finally, try to read between the lines and understand what is really going on. I have interviewed hundreds of people in my life for various positions, and my best advice to you when preparing for any interview question is to try and understand what the interviewer is really asking or testing. If you can get into the habit of going deeper and getting to the actual interest of a situation, rather than getting stuck with the words at the high level, you will perform much better.

Let me give you an example. If you are asked in an interview, "If you were an animal, what animal would you be?" What would you say? Take your eyes off of this book for twenty seconds and have a think.

The most common answers are a dog, because "I'm so loyal" (which does beg the question: *Why are you at this interview and not with your current employer*?); a wolf, because "I like working in teams"; or a lion, because "I'm the leader in the jungle." The underlying purpose of this question is to consider a stereotypical view of an animal and relate an analogy to describe one of your key characteristics.

I have heard some of the silliest answers to this question. I had one candidate who said to me that they would like to be a unicorn. This made me perk up and certainly got my attention, as it is not a common answer. I probed as to why, and the candidate responded, "It would be cool to have all of those colors." It was very difficult for me not to laugh, because the candidate had completely missed the point of the question. If they had said they wanted to be a unicorn because it was unique, it would have been passable.

In a similar vein, I had one person who responded with a bird. Now, a bird is usually quite a good answer; it means you like to take the aerial view to understand the big picture before settling on a decision. An eagle is often cited as a more specific example for the same reason. But when I asked this person, "Why a bird?" they responded with, "It would be cool to fly." I nearly fell off my chair. I wondered what on earth was going through their head, because this was a serious interview. I felt like explaining, "Look, I didn't ask you what animal you would like to be because I have a magic wand and will change you!" But what happened was simply that they took the question too literally. They did not understand the underlying purpose of the question, and instead only looked at the surface. Make sure you dig to the deeper level to find out what is really going on, and what is really being asked.*

A final example of digging deeper to find out how to answer questions in an interview comes from Larry Page, one of the cofounders of Google, who is noted for giving the directive, "Teach me something I don't know." Again, put this book down for one minute and consider how you would respond.

What do you think is really being tested here? Larry is

---

* The best answer that I have heard for the animal question is a duck. Why? "Because on the surface I am calm, but underneath the water, I am usually kicking like crazy." Great analogy, and it answers the deeper purpose of the question well.

cofounder of one of the most successful organizations ever, and I doubt he really wants to cram more information into his brain from something he learned in an interview. What is really being tested are your communication skills, your ability to be concise, and your ability to explain a fairly complex concept in simple terms that everyone can comprehend. If you understand the underlying reasoning for this question, then answering it becomes far easier.

The candidates who struggle are those who take the question too literally and do not understand its purpose. The thinking process will go along the lines of, "Oh no, teach you something that you don't know? What on earth do I know that you don't? You cofounded one of the most successful companies ever! I know, I will tell you a fun fact about my high-school mascot. I bet you didn't know that!" Of course, the candidate has completely missed the point and will not get the position.

My advice to you when you don't know what to say in response to an interview question is to ask for a moment to think. Now most people don't actually think of anything during this time. All they really do is beg in their mind, *Please, please, please, I hope some inspiration comes to me!* Well, now you know exactly what to think. You should be thinking, *What is the underlying purpose for this question? Why would anyone ask this question?*

BEING ENTREPRENEURIAL

> *"Build your own dreams, or someone will hire you to build theirs."*
>
> **—FARRAH GRAY**

When I talk to my undergraduate students about what they hope to achieve in the future, their answers are usually quite inspiring. They typically are, as yet, untainted by the rigors of finding a good career, and they see the future optimistically and with enthusiasm. However, I have noticed a disturbing trend of despair amongst this generation of students. They simply state that they cannot imagine how they can afford the kind of house or location that they would like to live in. At first, it seems to be an unnecessarily negative and pessimistic outlook, but on further clarification, it simply echoes realism.

Consider the following. As of the time of writing, where I live in Vancouver, beautiful British Columbia, Canada, the average salary is somewhere between (in Canadian dollars) $60,000 and $70,000, depending on what study you read. Let's take the midpoint of $65,000. The average price of a house in greater Vancouver is around $1.2 million (again, depending on which study you read). Current mortgage rules stipulate you must have 20 percent of a purchase price as an initial down payment. This means that you will need $240,000 just to put down as an initial payment.

Thereafter, you will be taking a mortgage out for close to a million dollars (plus, there are other closing costs that will need to be factored in). Even if you manage to snag a very low mortgage rate of, say, 4.5 percent, then you will still be paying at least $45,000 a year towards your interest payments. And this does not reduce your overall debt. With a salary of $65,000, you will only be taking home around $40,000 (after tax and other deductions). And remember, you still have to pay for all of your other expenses, such as food, clothes, travel, and so on.

The numbers just don't add up. Even if you save enough to afford a down payment and earn considerably more than the average worker, the mortgage will simply drain your funds. Even if you have two people working in your household, you will not come close to paying off your mortgage until you are well into your fifties or beyond.

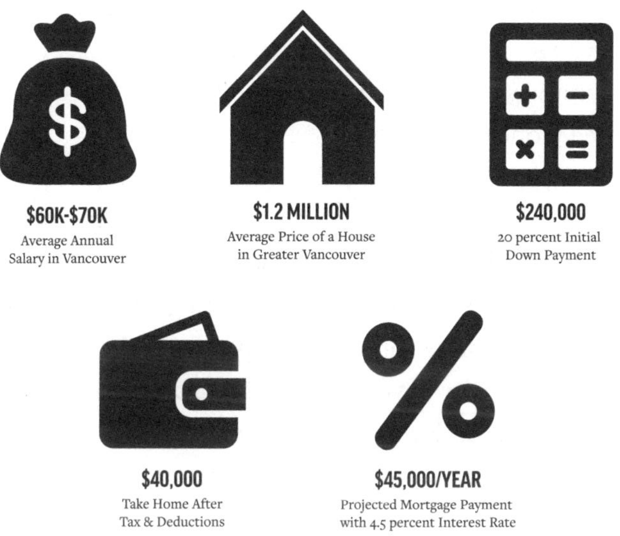

THE NUMBERS JUST DON'T ADD UP!

The above can seem disheartening, and I understand the despair. Similar situations are in place around the world in many other countries and regions. The question becomes, **What can you do about it?** How can you survive and thrive, especially if your occupation has clear ceilings in the salary that you can make?

When I mentor students, I advise the following. Do a job that you truly enjoy. Your enthusiasm for your vocation will ensure you excel at what you do, and you will keep your sanity by enjoying your work. You will also move towards the higher end of your salary scale because you will excel in your work because of your passion.

If the job does not pay enough, then you need to do something on the side that will make up the funds you need. Starting a small business or investing can help, often delivering results in the long term if you have patience. Opportunities may exist to take on separate jobs to secure multiple streams of income. The point is you need to be doing something else to make the required money. How can you be entrepreneurial?

Firstly, you need to think where there are problems or hassles. **Wherever there is a problem, there is an opportunity**. Many people do not like cooking or washing dishes, so there are a plethora of restaurants. People don't like getting out of their cars, so there are many drive-throughs. People don't like to wash their own clothes, so we have many laundry services. People don't want to mow their lawns or wash their windows or clean their gutters, so there are many people who get paid to provide these services. Whenever people don't want to do something or find something a hassle, there is an opportunity to do it en masse or more efficiently so that others will pay for the convenience.

What annoys you on a daily basis? What do you wish you didn't have to do? Extending this framework to organizations, what do you think is the number one most hated part of managers' jobs? That is correct: firing others. It is horrible because you feel that you have irrevocably affected those around you (and often, people you have known for a while), and morale tends to plummet in the organization amongst those who remain. Well, there are consultancies who will do the firing for you (watch the George Clooney movie *Up in the Air* for a good example). Looking for problems will help you find opportunities.

The Stone Age did not end because we ran out of stones. It ended because we discovered iron and bronze. Seek to innovate and make current practices obsolete. Where do you get the ideas from? **Travelling around the world is usually an eye-opener**. What do they do or have in other places that will work well where you are? There is never a perfect time to start a business (or move jobs, or start anything new). There are always reasons to maintain the status quo. Just do it anyway. Don't wait for perfection. Even if you try to make something idiot-proof, someone will merely make a better idiot.

Another method to think entrepreneurially is to think creatively to move into new space instead of thinking competitively. Chan Kim and Renée Mauborgne have done seminal work in this area with their development of the *Blue Ocean Strategy*. Briefly explained, if you compete in existing markets, you will face competitors who will fight you and end up turning the ocean (i.e., the marketplace) red with blood. Instead of this competition, try to move to unexplored spaces where there is a blue ocean with no direct competitors. You can then do very well, because it will take any future competitor a while to catch up.

Cirque du Soleil is a classic example of moving to a blue ocean. They did not win because they stole customers from traditional circuses, but because they invented a new form of entertainment: theatre blurred with acrobatics and a theme, which attracted new customers.

EXPANDING YOUR BUSINESS

Make sure you hire good people. If you hire mediocre people, they will hire mediocre people, and the cycle will be repeated. It takes talent to spot talent, and the good people will know what it takes in others to succeed. When looking for employees, **excitement is a better motivator than discipline**. The people who appear to have an exceptional work ethic or remarkable discipline are often those with a genuine curiosity or interest in that area. The person who smiles regularly is more likely to keep working than the person who is gritting their teeth. Try to surround yourself with good people. Lots of people want to ride with you in your jet, but what you want is someone who will take the economy fare with you when the jet breaks down.

If you take good care of your employees, they will take good care of your customers. On the subject of customers, make sure you listen to them regularly. In fact, your worst customers will often provide the very best insights. It is partly because we are more likely to complain when we are upset rather than give praise when we are satisfied. It is your job to look for patterns. If one person says something, then it may be an anomaly and/or they may not be reasonable with their complaint. But if several people say the same thing, then you must listen and correct at least the perception of your organization.

When it comes to sales, be very careful with the words you use. We all have certain connotations and thoughts in our minds when we hear different words, and you need to be aware of how they make people feel. For example, in sales, instead of using "cost" or "price," use the word "investment" when talking to customers. Everyone would prefer an investment over a cost, and no one wants to focus on how much they are paying. Instead of talking about a "contract," which invokes legal frameworks or suing, use the words "partnership" or "agreement," which invoke mutual benefits. Instead of "buy," use "own"; no one likes to buy things, but everyone likes to own—buying things is a pain, but owning is a pleasure.

Finally, a cautionary note to finish this chapter on money:

> *"Many people take no care of their money till they come nearly to the end of it, and others do just the same with their time."*
>
> **—JOHANN WOLFGANG VON GOETHE**

SUMMARY AND KEY LEARNING POINTS

- Money is extremely important. You need to learn how to handle money properly to support your endeavours in life.
- Consider what you would do if you came into a lot of money. Can you do any of those things today at a smaller scale?
- Money can provide freedom in some dimensions, but make sure it doesn't take away your freedom in others.
- You need to draw some boundaries and not just keep working towards more. There will always be people who have greater financial wealth than yourself.
- Financial wealth is just one type of wealth to look for. Other types of wealth include (and are not limited to) social wealth, physical wealth, time wealth, emotional wealth, and spiritual wealth. Increasing one type of wealth will often increase other types, but be careful not to cannibalize one wealth by increasing another.

- The money you gain can be split into four buckets: spending, saving, investing, and giving away. The ratios of the buckets can be adjusted as your financial situation evolves.
- The very best things in life are free. There are things that money simply cannot buy.
- Working hard will not only guarantee your best chance of having enough money to do what you want but will make you feel that you are making the most of your time.
- Try to add value by giving people more than what they ask for.
- When you do what you enjoy, there are not enough hours in the day. Conversely, when you don't enjoy what you are doing, there are too many hours in the day.
- Learning how to say no properly will help you on many occasions in life. It will help free up time and space to say yes to more important things.
- Do what you really enjoy. If you don't make enough money, consider supplemental income that will allow you to do what you want to do in life.
- To become entrepreneurial, consider problems or hassles that people go through and how you can serve their needs better.
- Surround yourself with great people. You can't possibly do everything yourself, and the great people will lift you to unimagined heights.
- Be careful of the words you use, particularly when trying to sell something. For a customer, *buying* things is a pain, but *owning* things is a pleasure.

Exercises

BUDGETING

To understand money, you need to first have a good grip on how you currently use money. This will allow you to make deliberate decisions on how to deploy money in the future. Creating a budget can be a straightforward and useful way to plan for expenses and help put yourself in a better financial position. Knowing where you currently spend money can raise awareness to cut unnecessary expenses and save for larger financial goals.

Over the next month, keep a journal of how you spend. You must include every penny that leaves yourself. The most common expenses (and you may choose to organize your journal with the following categories) are:

- Rent/mortgage
- Utility bills, such as heating, cooling, electricity, gas, water, and sewer
- Car/transportation, including gas, fares, parking, and tolls
- Groceries and toiletries, including food and drink
- Internet, TV, streaming, and cell phone services
- Travel, going out, and entertainment
- Clothes and other occasional purchases
- Debt and retirement (if applicable)

Note, the above list is not exhaustive, and you should tailor for your situation. Once you have completed the journal, you should not only feel more comfortable in how you actually use money, but you should also be able to spot patterns that will give clues to changes that could be made in your lifestyle to accommodate your budget. You can then set targets for future months, factoring in that there are often one-off expenses you will need to accommodate. The more aware you are of how you use money, the more likely you will be able to look after it.

USING MONEY

There are two exercises here to stimulate how you think about money.

EXERCISE A

If you are currently earning money through a job or business, fill out the first row of the table below with the approximate percentages of how you are assigning the income to each bucket. If you are not currently earning money, you can skip to the next step.

	SPENDING %	SAVING %	INVESTING %	GIVING AWAY %
Current				
Ideal				

Now, consider how you would fill out the second row, "Ideal." Note, this exercise is highly personal, and there is no right or wrong response. The purpose is to make you aware of your current situation and how close (or far) you are from your ideal situation. Your ideal may also change over time (for example, as you earn more), and thinking of these buckets will help you feel confident that you are using your money wisely.

EXERCISE B

What would you do if you won $10 million? More explicitly, consider the following questions:

- How would you change your life? How much of what you would change can actually be enacted now?
- How much of the $10 million would you allot to the four buckets of spending, saving, investing, and giving away?
- What would you purchase within the next year?
- Outside of purchases, what would you *do* in the next year?
- What would you invest in?
- Whom would you give away your money to?
- Would you change your job (if you have one) or your career trajectory?

The purpose of this exercise is to get you thinking about how you would handle lots of money, and to develop a wealthy mindset. The main point is in the details, that is, what *specifically* you would do. Like anything in life, the more you think about something, the more likely it is to occur.

WEALTH

Consider the following six types of wealth, and rate each one on a scale of 1 to 10, where 1 means that you feel you have little to none of this type of wealth, and 10 means that you feel you are positively overflowing with abundance in this type of wealth.

- **Financial wealth**—your assets, possessions, and overall net worth
- **Social wealth**—your status or title within your community, work, or school
- **Physical wealth**—your overall health
- **Time wealth**—your freedom to spend time as you wish
- **Emotional wealth**—the strength and number of your relationships
- **Spiritual wealth**—how content you are with your life and your purpose

The purpose of this exercise is to make you aware of where you are already wealthy and of which areas of your life you need to concentrate on. It is highly challenging to rate highly on all of the wealth types, but this should be your goal. Remember, it is the journey to get there that is important, and not the destination itself.

GETTING TO INTERESTS

A fundamental concept in negotiation (and more broadly, communication) is to get down to interests and not get stuck with positions. What is the difference?

A **position** is what you say you want. It could be a request, an offer, a demand, and so on, and is one of the many solutions to a situation.

An **interest** is what you really want—it is the underlying reason or desire for negotiating in the first place, and it helps define the problem to be solved.

For example, if I make an offer to purchase your laptop, my position may be that I offer you $1,000. However, my interest could be that I need a machine to work on whilst travelling. The interest is why I am *really* negotiating.

Great negotiators will always try to get to interests and not get stuck on positions. The concept is valid for communication as well. To understand others, we should try to get down to what others really mean with the words that they use.*

For example, if I say, "This is going to be a little challenging," I could mean everything from "It's going to require a bit of effort" all the way to "There is no way in the world this is possible."

The exact interests of anyone you communicate with are going to be dependent on the situation, the context, the history, the personality, and many other factors. However, you need to develop an awareness of the range of interests that someone may have. If you close your mind and think of only how you would interpret words, you could be missing out on understanding what is really going on. Try to fill out the following table with what the extremes of interests could be:

---

* As an aside, I find the difficulty of interpreting others varies depending on the culture you are in. Australians, for example, are typically quite blunt and straightforward with how they express themselves, and you often don't have to guess what they really mean. The British are at the other end of the scale, with more subtleness and understated language, which can prove harder to decipher the true meaning from.

PHRASE	LOWER EXTREME OF INTEREST	UPPER EXTREME OF INTEREST
"This is going to be a little challenging."	It's going to require a bit of effort.	There is no way in the world this is possible.
"That is nice."		
"I want to help you."		
"Well done."		
"I will get to this right away."		
"All the best."		
"That is interesting."		
"This is silly."		

("Interesting" is one of the most difficult words to decipher when someone uses it to describe something. It could mean almost anything!)

REFRAMING TO HELP SALES

As mentioned several times in this book, the words you use and how you frame conditions have a significant influence on how you interpret situations and your subsequent behaviour. The key is to try and frame them in a way that is helpful towards your goals. For example, if you are selling something, it is better to communicate to a buyer that they will *own* the good rather than *buy* the good. Buying is a pain, and owning is a pleasure.

In the table below, practice reframing the situation into something that is more positive or more likely to help you achieve your goals:

ORIGINAL SITUATION	REFRAMED IN A MORE POSITIVE LIGHT
Would you like to **buy** this good?	Would you like to **own** this good?
Cost or price	Investment
Contract	Partnership or agreement
Expenses	
Someone or something that is old	
Someone or something that is immature	
Far away	
Too close	
Unqualified	
Overqualified	
Too expensive	
Too cheap	
Too big	
Too small	
Too advanced	
Too basic	

REFLECTION QUESTIONS

- When is the last time you completely lost yourself in an endeavour, so much so that you didn't even remember to eat?
- What are all of the good causes that you would like to donate money and time to?
- If money was not an issue, what would your typical day look like? How about a typical month, or a typical year?
- Think of any financially wealthy person that you know (who made it themselves and did not inherit their fortune). How did they make their money? What contributed most to their success?
- What accomplishments are you most proud of? What, specifically, did you learn along the way?

CHAPTER 7

SPIRITUALITY AND FAITH

"Spirituality is recognizing and celebrating that we are all inextricably connected to each other by a power greater than all of us, and that our connection to that power and to one another is grounded in love and compassion. Practicing spirituality brings a sense of perspective, meaning and purpose to our lives."

—BRENÉ BROWN

Please do the following exercise right now. Put down this book and consider for thirty seconds the following question: "Why are you here?"

How did you find that question? Did you have any concrete ideas? Are you still thinking about the question now? In my mind, answering this question is really the core for learning about spirituality and faith. People who can answer this question confidently and with all their heart will feel what I call the 3 C's: Calm, Content, and Confident. They will face the world and all of its challenges with a quiet, unassuming manner. When they are happy, they will feel overjoyed, because they understand at a deep level what their purpose is. One test to measure spiritual evolution is to face adversity and not give up or be as affected as others because you know what is really important, and the adversity is not it.

I don't pretend to have all the answers, and I certainly cannot tell you what is good or bad or right or wrong in the bigger picture. I have my beliefs, and they may be very different from yours. I can share my observations, though, and I encourage you to read this chapter with an open mind. You may not agree with everything I say, and indeed, some of what you read may wholly conflict with what you have always believed. That is OK; consider it all part of your spiritual journey. Spirituality is a broad concept with room for many perspectives, and there are certainly many, many paths to become more enlightened. We will start with the concept of God.

GOD

> *"Suffering is the medicine, and pleasure the disease, because where there is pleasure, there is no desire for God."*
>
> **—GURU NANAK DEV JI**

Who or what is God? Is there even a God? Why do we have so many interpretations of what God is? Is there a magical force that pervades our Universe? Does God ensure that everything happens for a reason? These are difficult questions that have puzzled people since the beginning of mankind. There are no easy answers that can be universally accepted, and I believe this is intentional. We simply would not learn lessons the same way if we knew the answers. On a similar note, we would not live our lives in exactly the same way if we knew for sure what happens when we die. Most of us have absolutely no recollection of what we were or what we did in previous lives, because we would not learn the lessons from this life to the same degree if we did.

For some, it helps to think of God as some large mysterious being that is looking over everyone and everything and ensuring the universal laws (however you interpret them) are being applied. Some like to think of God as more of an energy rather than an actual being. I don't think it matters how you represent God in your mind, for it is unlikely that you will truly find out within your lifetime. (This is called being agnostic; that is, you believe it is impossible to ever really find out.) There are some who don't believe in God at all (atheists), and I disagree with this notion.

When I think of life (both the lives of others and my own), I can recall numerous instances that didn't seem to be random. Some would put these situations down to serendipity (happy accidents), but I just cannot believe that they were quirks of luck. Consider the following examples:

- Meeting exactly the right person at exactly the right time to help you in your life (maybe a partner, a colleague, or any other person).
- Receiving unexpected assistance in a task by having things fall your way.
- Realizing a strange feeling, which has absolutely no reason and no instigating force, at the last minute that helps you avoid a dangerous or negative situation.

Where do all of these examples come from? If they only happened very occasionally, then fine, I could see how chance could play a part. However, they seem to happen so regularly that I just cannot get my head around there not being some other things going on that we simply cannot fathom. When you consider the same things happen to billions of people around the world, and how our lives are so linked and affecting so many others around us, the complexity becomes astounding.

Personally, I believe that everyone belongs to a "Spiritual Group," and some of these spirits are having an animal experience with you (maybe the closest people in your life), and others are in what we can call the "spirit world." These spirits come into your life regularly and will help you in ways that we cannot imagine. Who looks after these spirits? I believe this is a God of some form.

The purpose of your Spiritual Group is to help one another learn lessons and evolve along spiritual dimensions. Hardships are sent your way to help you learn, and your Spiritual Group can interject both directly (through others who are also having an animal experience), and indirectly from the spiritual world. If something happens to you that helps your life, and you have absolutely no idea where it came from, it just may have come from someone in your Spiritual Group who recognized your path needed to be reinforced. For example, an unexpected encounter with a complete stranger that changes your life. Or a very bad feeling about a situation that drives you to change direction and unknowingly, without any logic, avoid a disaster.

What happens when we die? The answer to this question varies tremendously depending on what you believe. Reincarnation, or coming back as another life (possibly animal or human) is believed by some. Others believe nothing happens—you simply die, and that is it. The reason I do not believe the "nothing" answer (and do believe in reincarnation) is that I just can't imagine that, given the millions of years that have already passed and the likely millions of years of the future, we have the ridiculous average of only eighty years or so for our life. Surely there has to be more to each of our existences than that!

Death can be a tough topic to think about. Along with taxes, it is the only thing guaranteed for all of us. **Most people want to concentrate on living rather than considering what happens when we die**. As you get older, you tend to think more about death (because you know of more people around you who die, and because you appreciate you are getting closer to that day yourself!). If you take a spiritual view of life, you don't worry so much about death. If you believe our spirits are eternal, then contemplating death becomes far easier because you will believe the people that you know and love do not actually die, but rather, they stop having this temporary human existence.

I believe what the French philosopher Pierre Teilhard de Chardin said: "We are not human beings having a spiritual experience. We are spiritual beings having a human experience." Our lives as we know them will only last for an average of about eighty years. But the spirit that drives us is, I believe, eternal. Given that our spirit is eternal, I believe we are all parts of God. This is why it makes no sense to harm others, as, in effect, you are harming other eternal parts of God. Try not to be angry at anything, particularly other people. **Everything is a manifestation of God and exists for a purpose**. If you get angry at anything, you are, in fact, getting angry at God, and that cannot be good.

Try to embrace the positives and seek reasons as to why things happen. Often, when you get angry at someone else, you are actually letting out some of your own frustrations. For example, when driving, if you feel very good or are talking nicely to a loved one, then another driver who performs a dangerous or irritating act will not bother you so much. However, if you are late or stressed, then you may well react with anger or road rage. God frequently tests you, especially when you feel down. The key is to try and keep a peaceful and calm mind as often as possible. When you get angry, you hurt yourself far more than whatever you are angry at. Remember, anger is just one letter short of danger.

Don't seek to punish people or look for revenge, because Karma has its own magnificent way of balancing things out. What I have learned about Karma is that it is very indirect. If you trip me on purpose to embarrass and hurt me in front of others, this does not mean that in the future, Karma will ensure you get tripped in front of others. More likely, the *way* you made me *feel* is what will come back to you. It may occur in a completely different context or situation, but those feelings I had of hurt and embarrassment will be yours.

Now, please bear in mind there are many that disagree with the concepts I have described, and that is OK. I believe it is important for you to ask questions and figure out in your own mind what is going on. Being agnostic can be seen as being humble, because you are admitting you cannot know anything for sure given the lack of proof. And I believe that if you don't believe in anything, you are missing out on one of the most inspiring and uplifting practices possible. When you have a strong belief in who or what God is, then you will have this concept driving you in almost all situations. Your belief in this higher power feels almost mystical. It will help you get over the worst of the worst and will give your life a strong and powerful purpose. If God is with you, then who could possibly be against you?

RELIGION

Religion is one of the most powerful, yet also one of the most dangerous, things in the world. Why? **Because religion provides people with remarkable *belief*.** When you believe something 100 percent, it can supply you with power that is otherwise unobtainable. Looking back at our previous section, belief in God gives you confidence that everything happens for a reason. You can build a level of positive ambivalence (being immune to how things turn out) because you believe it is all for a purpose and the higher power is helping you. If you don't know where you are going, then any road will get you there, because you won't know the difference.

Having read several of the famous religious texts (the Guru Granth Sahib, the Bible, the Torah, the Quran, the Tipitaka, the Tao Te Ching, the Vedas, the Upanishads, and the Bhagavad Gita), I see that every major religion has taken different directions with God, our purpose, what is important, and so on. What struck me most, however, was not the differences but the similarities in what was written. The texts are not congruent, but they have far more in common than they do differences. As a child, what always puzzled me was how there could be so many religions all claiming to deepen our understanding of God, our purpose, and way of being, yet they didn't agree. Which one was correct, if any? Even more puzzling would be how people could change the religion they follow. Were their previous beliefs valid? Why were their new beliefs now more important to them?

I realized over time the reason for these anomalies stemmed from the fact that religion is man-made. These texts have been written by and interpreted by humans. I don't pretend to know definitively how the texts came into being, but I do know they are extremely powerful and have helped billions of people over time. And that is the key—religion can be very, very helpful, because it helps bestow staggering levels of belief.

Religion is not spirituality, but it can be an excellent start to your spiritual journey. It is a prescription to help you achieve spirituality in the future. If you were not spiritual at all, then it would be very difficult to learn all of the things necessary to become spiritual without knowledge of religion. If you have no clue as to how to start becoming more spiritual, then religion is very helpful. It provides all kinds of signposts that assist you in your journey. Use religion wisely; do not blindly believe and follow every nuance. If a person's religion makes them more whole and inspires them to achieve greater feats and true happiness, then it works.

Religion gives us hope, belief, and an understanding of a force greater than we can imagine—all essential components of spirituality. But most importantly, *being religious does not equate to being spiritual.* I believe that religion can only take you to a certain point. Beyond that, becoming more spiritual (that is, more attuned to God or a higher power) is attained in a very personal way. Again, religion can help, but it is not the only way. When we come to the realization that we are all equal and no better or worse than anyone else, the foundations of some religions start to falter. How can some people believe contrasting things simply because of the religion they were born (or converted) into? Studying different religions brings you insight. Following your curiosity and learning how others view their purpose will reap multiple rewards in advancing your own spiritual practice.

A central tenet to many religions is what we call "the Golden Rule." This notion refers to treating others how you would like to be treated. Indeed, we are reminded of this below:

> *"That which is hateful to you, do not do to your fellow. This is the whole Torah; all the rest is commentary."*
>
> **—HILLEL THE ELDER**

Given this concept is repeated in so many ways and from so many different sources, I think it is one of the best suggestions that we should all live by.

BEING SPIRITUAL

I have found that being nice and doing things for others without any desire for reciprocation are some of the best ways to develop your own spirituality. When you help others unconditionally, it simply feels good. When you help an old person cross a street, it just makes you feel good inside. On the other hand, when you lie or cheat someone, you feel a little twist inside. It is almost as if we all have an internal barometer telling us, "Do these things and you will feel good," and "Don't do those things, otherwise you will feel bad." When you do things without asking for anything in return, you feel connected to a deeper power, which raises your spiritual awareness, for you know you are doing good, but don't need a direct, understandable reward in return. Instead, you are learning the very important practice of letting go and ambivalence.

For some of us, our barometers are a little twisted, but we all have them. The problem is that you can only hear your barometer when you have silence or peace inside. True intelligence also comes from this silence. Seek silence if you can. Like muscles, these barometers will get stronger the more you use (listen) to them, and you should try to do so immediately. The fruit of unwavering service is peace. Funnily enough, giving doesn't count when you don't want what you give away. You are, in effect, discarding rather than giving. When you seek silence, you make room for calmer, different thoughts that can stimulate curiosity (see chapter on Learning), and promote longer-term peace.

I was raised in the Sikh religion, and one concept that gets repeated constantly is Seva. Seva is the idea of selfless service performed without any expectation of reward, or in other words, dedication to others. The principles of Seva underpin many Sikh values, and I was taught from a young age the importance of Seva to cultivate a spiritual mind. Around the world, wherever you see Sikhs, you will notice Seva; for example, in providing food for the hungry or needy without prejudice. It is a wonderful practice that I believe moves you closer to God. Be a servant to others, for what we do for ourselves dies with us, but what we do for others in the world remains and is immortal.

You are surrounded by people who influence every part of your life, so be kind. Try to leave people better than you found them. It's not just about saying the right things, but doing the right things that counts. It doesn't matter if they can hear you or not; try not to talk negatively about anyone. **If you have nothing good to say, then say nothing**. Be very careful of the words you use to describe others, and make your words loving and tender, because you may just have to eat them tomorrow.

When you are positive about others, even if they are not present, you build character, and building character is far more important than achieving results. You want to get into the habit of doing more than just listening to others; instead, seek to understand what they really mean. Put yourself in their shoes. How would you behave and react to situations if you had been through everything that they have? **The compassionate mindset will help you understand, grow, and be the kind of person that others want to help and be around.**

When people do things that you do not like, you must strive to forgive them as soon as possible. Most people have a terrible problem with forgiving. They believe that if you forgive someone, you are admitting that the other person was "right." Nothing could be further from the truth. You do not forgive people to acknowledge that they may have been correct. Rather, forgiveness is an entirely selfish pursuit. You forgive people so that you can let go and move on. If you do not forgive them, then they have a hold on you, even from a very long distance. Every time you think about them or the situation, you get a little tight inside. When you forgive them, you can let go of any anger and blame and return to your inner balance and peace.

The funny thing is that you do not even have to tell others that you are forgiving them. You can just forgive them in your own mind. (There can be value to forgiving them in person, and you can use your discretion as to whether this is a wise action.) The heaviest thing that you can carry around with you is a grudge. I think Paul Boese put it best when he said, "Forgiveness does not change the past, but it does enlarge the future." Besides, hate is baggage, and life is simply too short to be upset all the time. Do not forget to forgive yourself, for we are often our own worst enemies. If you keep telling yourself that you were silly and made big mistakes, then your 3 C's (Calm, Contentment, and Confidence) plummet.

All of these practices—giving without any thought of return, forgiving, focusing on positives, and being nice—will elevate your spiritual sentience. You will become a calmer, more confident and contented being whom others will seek guidance from, because you will be living and demonstrating firsthand the value and results of leading a spiritual life. Others will see the quiet glow and strength that you will exhibit. As Saint Francis de Sales put it so eloquently: "Nothing is so strong as gentleness, nothing so gentle as real strength."

When making decisions, being more spiritual means that you use your heart more than your head. I was sitting next to an old

Russian lady on a flight from London to Milan, and she gave me some wonderful advice that has stuck with me. She said to follow your heart. Your head is full of training, logic, and what you have learned from others—that is, what *they* say. Your heart is full of your soul and has not been polluted. Follow your heart. What wonderful words. I have found that when we are making any complex, nontrivial decisions, it works best to follow your heart. When making simple decisions, lots of analysis may make sense.

Don't think too much about complex decisions. The more you think, the more reasons you will come up with to do something or not do something, and you will get more confused. The more people you talk to, the more conflicting advice you will get, and the result will be even more confusion. Follow your gut instinct. Nine times out of ten, it is correct, and the one time it is not—well, who cares? You did what you felt was right at the time. If you overanalyze, you end up with what we call "analysis paralysis," which not only makes deciding more difficult but also guarantees remorse, that is, regret, about the final decision. Listen to your gut feeling. Your gut feeling is not random. It is a sum of all your experiences in this life (and if you believe in this, previous lives too). If it doesn't feel right to you, it probably isn't. Your levels of intuition will also increase when you listen to your heart more and will decrease if you ignore it.

Listening to your heart also forces you to delve into deep introspection. Several philosophers believe that your life is simply a direct reflection of your inner self. Everything you experience on the outside is a mirror image of your innermost thoughts, feelings, and beliefs. Therefore, to change anything on the outside, you have to look inside first. If you believe the world is a horrible place and full of horrible people, that is probably what you will notice.

It's worth talking a little bit about time. **Everything happens for a reason.** It is not always easy to see, but eventually, things become clear. Your spirit, which does not work in the conventional time that we are accustomed to, has already decided what lessons you must learn to grow and fulfill your destiny. You live out those lessons and would not learn otherwise. Therefore, have faith that no matter what happens, it happens for the best.

Another way of looking at time is to consider how precious it is. We can lose many things in life, and get them back. We can lose money, or material possessions, and get them back. We can even lose relationships to a certain degree, and get them back. But time, once it is gone, is never to return. Today will never come again. You will never be in the exact same place at the same time again. This is why you need to choose *where* and *whom* you spend your time with carefully, and cherish every moment with loved ones.

Yet another way of looking at time comes from Ayurveda, which is the traditional Hindu system of medicine that relies on balance. According to Ayurveda, every human being is the **environment, body, mind,** and **spirit** woven together.

The **environment** has the shortest shelf life, for it is changing every moment. The **body** has a slightly longer shelf life. It takes about seven to ten years to replace almost all the atoms and molecules that compose it.

The **mind**, which includes the intellect and ego, has a still longer shelf life. Your aspirations, beliefs, dreams, memories, and desires may last an entire lifetime. Your **spirit** is eternal and not subject to the entropy and decay that govern the environment, body, and mind.

Live your life from the level of your soul, and you will be timeless.

If you are not moving to the next desired stage in life, or if you feel there is some kind of blockage, consider, from purely a spiritual point of view, the following two questions: What have you not learned? Why? This presupposes you believe life is a progression of learnings and our deeper purpose is to develop and fulfill potential. Life is short, so do the right thing. If you err in any way, apologize immediately and move on.

LOOKING TO THE FUTURE

> *"Destiny is not a matter of chance; it is a matter of choice. It is not a thing to be waited for; it is a thing to be achieved."*
>
> **—WILLIAM JENNINGS BRYAN**

We make many, many decisions every single day. According to neuroscientists at Cornell University, the average adult makes over 35,000 decisions daily (with 226 just on food)! We are decision-intensive organisms, and our multitude of decisions have consequences. Given that we have power to make many decisions, why don't we make them more positively? You want to live your life by moving *towards* what you *want*, rather than *away* from what you *fear*. This is also the simplest framework we can use for motivation. Your motivation to do anything is either to move towards what you want or away from what you fear. Again, I find believing in God helps, because it makes you less fearful about the future and therefore more likely to concentrate on what you want.

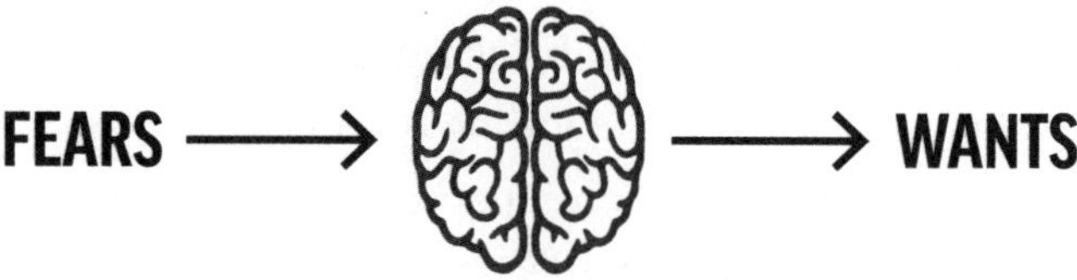

Choose a path that makes for a good story. Imagine sitting on your porch when you are in your nineties, surrounded by family members, and they ask you to tell them about your life. What would you like to say? You might as well let your imagination run wild now because if you have choices, why settle for a mediocre life? Why not go for an amazing, fulfilling, inspiring, and phenomenal life? Try to live without regret. Our regrets are usually for things that we *don't* do rather than for what we do. Every one of us will eventually die. That much is inevitable. The sad thing is that few of us actually get to live full and enriching lives. So few us really *live*. Indeed, our biggest fear is not of dying but of not living fully before we die. Why does making a good story help with your spirituality? It provides you with a sense of calm and contentment that all will be well in the future. It provides an optimistic future that you can look forward to and quietly builds your confidence to reach your goals.

As much as I have written about being nice to others, you have to realize that your time is finite, and you simply shouldn't waste it with people who are not helpful to your journey. If you argue too long with an idiot, then you begin to look like an idiot yourself! Some people try to appear taller by cutting off the heads of others. There are also what I call "ankle-grabbers." These are folks that will keep grabbing at your ankles to pull you down when you are trying to lift yourself and rise to new heights. We all experience inner conflicts, such as moral conflicts, whether we should tell a white lie, and other situations where we are torn between doing the right thing or the alternative (usually easier) thing. If you reduce these conflicts by deliberately making choices that are in line with your core beliefs, life becomes much smoother because your actions become more congruent and your beliefs grow stronger by being reaffirmed on a regular basis.

Try not to have too many attachments. Many religions preach the idea of not getting too attached to anything. The fewer attachments you have—to possessions, to people, and to your daily life—the less likely you will have expectations that lead to disappointment. Be free and have no attachments, and you will have inner peace to get through anything. **Do not become too attached to the things you like. Do not maintain aversion to the things you dislike**. Sorrow, fear, and bondage come from one's likes and dislikes.

I must admit that I find not having attachments to some things extremely difficult. I am not sure *exactly* how I would react, but if my children were removed from my life, I would likely be a mess. I am just too attached to them. Life is not what happens to you, but rather how you react. In this extreme situation, I think I would react in a very negative way. It's easy to speculate now, when the issues are not occurring, but if devastating things happen to you, the initial emotional reaction may be too big to circumvent. It will take time, but you have to try, no matter what, to have faith that all will be well and that the bigger picture is working in your favor.

Suffering is necessary until you realize that it is unnecessary. **Without suffering, you would have no depth as a person**. Suffering teaches you lessons you may otherwise not learn. But once you've learned them, the suffering will no longer be needed. The lesson has been learned and you can move on. Part of having strong faith is accepting these lessons without knowing for sure.

As I've mentioned, I love walking. It does not matter what the weather is, I will enjoy the walk. If it is sunny and warm, great. If it is cold, then I get to wear a nice warm jacket. If it is raining, then I feel great for the plants and trees that get a good soaking. If it is dark, then there are far fewer people out and about, and I can enjoy the solitude. The point is to try and remain calm and happy no matter what. If you keep wishing for things to be different, you will suffer many disappointments. As Epictetus reminds us: "Do not seek to have events happen as you wish, but wish them to happen as they do happen, and all will be well with you."

When you wish things to be different, you are, in effect, fighting nature. There is nothing wrong with hoping for a positive result. The issue comes when you are disappointed when things don't go your way. Developing a mindset of "Whatever will be, will be" and "All things happen for a good reason" may help in building your ambivalence. Note, you still try your best in all situations (don't simply leave everything up to fate), but once you've given it your all, you can be content with whatever the actual outcome is. This calmness allows you to face bigger challenges with a clear, focused, and alert mind. But if you wish things were different, you will likely become agitated and, worse, lose belief due to something that you cannot control. One of the most common words used to describe spiritually evolved beings is "calm." No matter the situation, their spirit is confident enough in the belief of "things will be how they are meant to be" to keep them calm.

If you have a confident outlook, you will be best placed to deal with the curveballs when they arrive. **If you are not confident, you will be insecure, and insecurity is the mother of greed.** Being strong and confident does not mean you have to be arrogant. Indeed, you must stay humble. William Shakespeare said it best when he wrote, "A fool thinks himself to be wise, but a wise man knows himself to be a fool."

That positive outlook will help you in many fields. If you *believe* something is easy, then it will feel that way. The concept works in the same way if you think something will be difficult or impossible. You set the scene and determine the process and outcome simply by framing it as such in your mind, even before an event or situation. See the glass half full and have an optimistic outlook. You don't know what is going to happen, so why not think in a way that is helpful and empowering? Remember that it is never too late to make things better. You may not be able to start again from scratch, but you can start now to make sure the ending is positive.

Finally, I would like to share a quote that I think sums up this chapter nicely. I encourage you to find quotes and references that resonate with you and will therefore help you understand your journey.

> "Our deepest fear is not that we are inadequate. Our deepest fear is that we are powerful beyond measure. It is our light, not our darkness, that most frightens us. We ask ourselves, Who am I to be brilliant, gorgeous, talented, fabulous? Actually, who are you not to be? You are a child of God. Your playing small doesn't serve the world. There is nothing enlightened about shrinking so that other people won't feel insecure around you.
>
> We are all meant to shine, as children do. As we let our own light shine, we unconsciously give other people permission to do the same. As we're liberated from our own fear, our presence automatically liberates others."
>
> —Marianne Williamson

SUMMARY AND KEY LEARNING POINTS

- Understanding why you are here and what your deeper purpose is, is the essence of being spiritually aware. The more aware you are, the more Calm, Content, and Confident you will be. These 3 C's strengthen your spirit by helping you have faith that things are working out how they are supposed to, even if they are outside of your control or understanding.
- God is interpreted in many ways, and your interpre-

tation is highly personal. I like to think of God as some form of energy that permeates all around us and is the source of everything we know. The reason I believe in God is because how else would all the beauty that surrounds us and the manner in which all of our lives are inextricably linked be possible?

- I believe we are spirits experiencing a temporary human existence. Our spirits do not die and are a part of God. To assist in our spiritual evolution, we all belong to Spiritual Groups, which consist of some spirits also having human existences (usually those closest to us) and spirits who are in the spirit world. The purpose of every life is to evolve along our spiritual journey.
- Death becomes easier to contemplate if you believe our spirits are eternal.
- Try to be positive and kind and to not succumb to anger or seek revenge. Be confident that everything is working out exactly how it is supposed to be, and that there are an infinite number of spiritual incidents occurring all around you that you cannot possibly fathom.
- Religion provides many signposts to help you evolve spiritually, most notably by instilling hope and belief in a higher power that is in control and doing what is best. Religion is not, however, spirituality.
- Practice Golden Rule behaviour; that is, treat others like you would like to be treated.
- Forgiveness is not about admitting that you were at fault, but more so a selfish practice that will

help you move on. Your spirit will then be unperturbed by any baggage or negative memories towards that person/situation.
- Follow your heart when you are making complex decisions. Thinking will give you lots of logical analysis, but using your heart taps into your soul, which is untainted and unbiased.
- Time is the one thing you can never get back. This day will never happen again. Choose how and where you spend your time wisely.

Exercises

RAISING KNOWLEDGE

Countless clues towards spirituality have been left to us from many beings and practices around the world and over time. The purpose of this exercise is to increase your knowledge and understanding of such practices to help feed your soul. When you have a great understanding and respect for religions and sacred practices, you will have a deeper well from which to draw insights, and you can figure out in your own mind what is really important.

Try to do as many of the following as you can:

- Read the sacred texts for different religions. There should be no problem getting translations of these texts for your native language. At a minimum, read the following texts of the major religions:
    - The Bible

- The Torah
- The Quran
- The Tipitaka
- The Tao Te Ching
- The Vedas
- The Upanishads
- The Bhagavad Gita
- The Guru Granth Sahib
- The Egyptian Book of the Dead

- When reading these texts, look for patterns and for what comes up again and again. Also, take your time—this is not an exercise to rush through and get to the end, but rather, one to help you stop and reflect to let it all sink in. Discuss the texts with those that you trust.
- Where possible, visit the holy places of religions that are close to you. Even better, go with someone who is well versed in that religion and seek a tour and explanations for the common practices. Places to visit include churches, cathedrals, temples, mosques, synagogues, shrines, and so on.
- Make it a habit to visit holy places on your travels and to understand the significance and history of such sites.

RAISING AWARENESS

Becoming more aware of your emotions can provide you with valuable perspective and insights that can foster personal growth and spiritual evolution. Your emotions are deeply personal and highly subjective. What annoys you to no end may have zero impact on someone right next to you. Understanding the different ways you get triggered and the frequency with which you experience certain emotions can heighten your ability to self-regulate and build emotional intelligence.

Over the next week, record in a journal the times when you feel the following emotions. Note, you do not have to record every instance, but rather, significant cases when the emotions were especially strong. It is probably best to complete this exercise at the end of every day:

- **Kindness**—Every time you are very kind to a person. Note, kindness can take many forms: being helpful, offering support, taking time to assist, and so on.
- **Joy**—Every time you feel intense happiness at anything.
- **Anger or disappointment**—Every time you get significantly angry or disappointed about any issue or person.
- **Fear or worry**—Every time you feel significant fear towards something or someone.
- **Grief or hurt**—Every time you feel grief or get hurt significantly by something or someone.
- **Injustice**—Every time you think something happens to or around you that just is not fair.

REFLECTING ON CORE QUESTIONS

Becoming more spiritually evolved requires you to contemplate deep concepts on a regular basis. There are no simple answers, and you cannot quickly come to conclusions. The journey itself is highly personal, and one that others cannot make for you. Sure, people can (and will) help, but you must get used to introspection.

Read one of the questions below each morning, and try to spend as much of the day thinking about that question. When you feel your mind wandering, gently bring it back to the task at hand. Think about the question on the way to school or work. Talk about the question with people around you. The point is that you want to spend as much discretionary time as you have in a single day just to ponder a single question. I love doing this exercise on the second half of my walks.

- **Question 1**—Why are you here?
- **Question 2**—What happens to us when we die?
- **Question 3**—Who or what is God? (And if you are an atheist, ask, How do you explain how our lives are so inextricably linked?)

The purpose of this exercise is to make you more aware of your own thoughts and beliefs, as well as to introduce other thoughts on these key topics of existence. You never know where the key insights that will support you in your life will come from.

LEGACY

The purpose of this exercise is to get you thinking about what you really want to accomplish in this life and how much of a difference you wish to make. The exercise may prove inspiring and demanding and will help provide guidance on where you should be focusing your efforts. Let your imagination run wild and try to concentrate on the positives of how you lived, rather than the sadness of passing. As Dr. Seuss so movingly reminds us: "Don't cry because it's over. Smile because it happened."

Imagine you have been tasked to write the speech that will be delivered at your funeral. It does not matter who will be delivering the speech. Make sure to include the following:

- A little bit about your history.
- Your greatest accomplishments.
- How you made a difference in the lives around you.
- What you did that will continue to benefit lives around you.
- All the positive qualities of your personality that anyone who knew you would attest to.
- Some incredible stories that sum you up nicely.

REFLECTION QUESTIONS

- Why are you here? What is your true purpose in life?
- How often do you think about your purpose?
- What does God mean to you?

- What are the three best and three worst things to ever happen to you? Can you see any patterns to figure out why?
- Given your experiences to date, who are the people that you believe are part of your Spiritual Group? Most people gravitate towards family members, but this group can include friends, neighbors, teachers, or anyone who has significantly helped you in life.
- If you had to choose, whom would you like to have in your Spiritual Group (folks who support you unwaveringly in your spiritual development, for this life and any other)?
- How do you feel most of the time? How would you like to feel most of the time? Why don't you feel that way all the time now?

CHAPTER 8

LEADERSHIP

"If your actions inspire others to dream more, learn more, do more, and become more, you are a leader."

—JOHN QUINCY ADAMS

I left leadership to the final chapter because once you have developed yourself, the ultimate goal is to inspire others to reach greater heights. **There is only so much you can achieve by yourself**, and a leader knows how to achieve remarkable heights by influencing those around them. Leadership is a massive topic that continues to grow year over year at a frightening rate. There are volumes of books dedicated to the subject. You can even take whole degree programs in leadership. What does leadership really entail? There are many definitions of leadership and many directions you can take it in. Don't measure leadership simply by how successful you are in a given area. Rather, measure it by how much you contribute back to the society and community that has allowed you to become a leader. I like to think of leadership as simply the ability to *influence* others to *achieve goals*. How do you measure leadership? By simply counting the number of followers you have and assessing the impact you have on them. As you become more of a leader, you will have more followers and more impact.

From what I have seen, the most important attribute for all leaders is **integrity**. If you say you are going to do something, you better follow through and do it. People will question everything about you as you evolve as a leader. They will question your experience, your judgement, your background, your ability, and so on. As you become more senior, you will have more questioners. But the one thing you never want people to question is your integrity. This is because leadership is not a popularity contest, but rather, a contest to gain respect.

It is impossible to please everyone. No matter what you do, there will always be people who do not like you. However, people will respect you if you have enough integrity, even if they do not like you. This respect is what gains you more followers who are willing to support you in your leadership endeavours. Doing the right thing does not always make you popular in everyone's eyes, but as long as you know that you have been equitable and selfless, then even your harshest critic will admire and respect your integrity. Your word is, after all, the one thing that you can give and still keep. Note, building your integrity and trustworthiness can take years, but these things can also be destroyed in seconds. Be careful.

Major accomplishments will take time. It is called the **ladder** of success for a reason. Success is not a one-shot affair; it requires taking many steps. Superstars in almost any field will tell you that "overnight success" actually takes about fifteen years! Even those who have reached the very pinnacle remind us of their failures. Michael Jordan, one of the greatest basketball players of all time, said, "I've missed more than nine thousand shots in my career. I've lost almost three hundred games. Twenty-six times I've been trusted to take the game-winning shot and missed. I've failed over and over and over again in my life. And that is why I succeed."

If you want to achieve marvelous feats, you have to be comfortable with failure. Leaders persist even when failure hits them repeatedly, while average people give up easily. You need to have faith that everything happens for a reason, and as the Dalai Lama tells us, "Remember that sometimes not getting what you want is a wonderful stroke of luck."

What do leaders actually do? In my mind, leaders have four chief responsibilities:

- **Provide direction**—Establish and communicate a vision for a team.
- **Take action**—Make strategic decisions, and manage conflict and change.
- **Encourage**—Provide guidance and mentorship to support their followers.
- **Go beyond**—Think creatively to problem-solve and guide others.

We will frame the rest of the chapter around these four themes.

PROVIDE DIRECTION

"The single biggest problem in communication is the illusion it has taken place."

"In the right key one can say anything. In the wrong key, nothing: the only delicate part is the establishment of the key."

—GEORGE BERNARD SHAW

The starting point of all leadership is to establish goals and to craft a vision. A vision is an ideal picture of the future if everything goes as planned. What do you really want to achieve? What does a bright future look like? How will you know when you get there? Great leaders are visionary and can clearly define the high-level goals for any situation. All organizations need direction. When people feel lost, it's often because the overall goals/vision are not clear (or have not been communicated well).

To provide direction, you need ideas. Where do you get the ideas from? Your board, advisors, mentors, and senior folk who have wisdom are great to plan and strategize with and bounce ideas off of. These people will make sure you go in the right direction and that your momentum is suitably channeled by avoiding high-level pitfalls.

You must not worry about what others think when you are developing lofty goals. Sure, get the input from trusted people to help craft the goals, but once established, do not let the naysayers put you off. Keep going, for the road to success is dotted with many tempting parking places and many traffic police to grind you to a halt. The key with all messaging is to engage other people's hearts and emotions. Maya Angelou put it charmingly when she said, "I've learned that people will forget what you said, people will forget what you did, but people will never forget how you made them feel." This is true for all types of communication, and it's why you should leave people better than you found them.

Coming up with novel ideas can be difficult. Have you ever heard of the five monkeys experiment? Imagine putting five monkeys in a room with a ladder beneath a beautiful bunch of ripe bananas. Now, the first monkey tries to climb the ladder but, along with the other monkeys, is immediately pelted with icy water. So, no monkey climbs the ladder. Now imagine you take one monkey out and put a new one in. The new monkey sees the bananas, wants the bananas, but also sees no one else is climbing the ladder and figures there must be a reason. Now imagine taking the monkeys out one by one, replacing old ones with new ones. Eventually, you will have a room full of monkeys, with none climbing the ladder, and more importantly, none of them knowing *why*.

"Because we have always done it this way" is the answer you get when you ask most governments or bureaucratic organizations why they do things the way they do. So, break the mould and try something new. Don't be blinded or biased by previous solutions. As Wayne Gretzky, one of the greatest hockey players of all time told us about anticipation: "I skate to where the puck is going to be, not where it has been." Where is the puck in your world going to be in the future? Look at the key underlying trends and make sure your ideas are harmonious with those trends.

Keep it simple. Succinct communication of your message, (and indeed succinct communication in general) is always better than using big words.

FOR FUTURE LEADERS

One of the biggest mistakes I see recent graduates make is the desire to impress their management with long words and complex sentences to make themselves appear more intelligent. Rest assured, if you used a thesaurus to dress up your communication, I will likely need a dictionary to decipher it! Managers want to understand your message quickly and clearly and do not want to be blinded by indirect language. There is a reason why most reports have some form of summary. Readers will look at the summary, and if it is clear, inspiring, and to the point, they can choose if they want to read the rest of the report.

If you can touch people's hearts and not just their minds with your messaging, they are far more likely to follow you enthusiastically. Getting to their hearts means that you are getting to their emotions. Getting to their heads is providing reason. **The prime difference between emotion and reason is that emotion leads to action, while reason leads to conclusions**. You want to make people feel like they are making a difference and not just running in a rat race. Lily Tomlin put it beautifully when she said, "The trouble with the rat race is that even if you win, you're still a rat." If this is how you feel, then maybe you are running in the wrong type of race.

It is worth spending a little time at the beginning to make sure your goals and messaging are durable and suitable. It is better to be at the bottom of a ladder that you want to climb than halfway up a ladder you don't. A great analogy I like to think of is being tasked to run through a forest in front of you. The worst thing you can do is just start running. If you do so, you will likely get turned around, lost, and frustrated in the long run. The better initial action is to climb the first tree you see, take a good look at the entire landscape, and then plot a suitable course. It will take more time at the beginning but save you lots of time, energy, and sanity later on. Take the same approach with confirming your goals, since everything else will stem from them. We don't know what will happen in the future, but the best way to predict the future is to create it yourself with your goals.

Focus is important when you are narrowing down your ideas. As our old friend Confucius reminds us: "The man who chases two rabbits catches neither." Within leadership (and life in general), it is usually quite easy to say yes. In the art of leadership, though, it is much harder to say no. No to people, no to ideas, no to paths forward. By agreeing to do some things, you are also saying no to others. **By reading this book, you are simultaneously deciding not to do any of the other billion things that you could be doing at this moment.** I am forever grateful to you for you making that choice, and this mentality will help you to say no when needed.

Don't worry about others shooting down your ideas. The source of pessimism and skepticism is usually fear: fear of something going wrong, fear of ridicule, fear of what might happen to one's own position, and so on. **You want to be one of the few that do rather than the many that talk**. I've lost count of the number of people I've met who talk about starting a business, talk about climbing the corporate ladder, talk about making a difference, but end up not taking any action to get there. They resign themselves to hoping fate will interject and propel them to the promised land. This is not you. You will take action and do something.

TAKE ACTION

> *There are three types of people in this world:*
> *Those who make it happen. (Leaders)*
> *Those who let it happen. (Followers)*
> *Those who wonder what happened. (The Lost)*
>
> **—ADAPTED FROM NICHOLAS MURRAY BUTLER**

To succeed, you need to think of more than just the lofty goals and vision discussed in the previous section. **You need both ideas**

and implementation. You can dream all you like, but unless you have people doing things, your dreams will remain exactly that: dreams. Your implementers are people who do the actual work. They will do the day-to-day tasks, so they need to be efficient and have appropriate tools to excel in their jobs.

Some would describe the ideas and direction piece as being performed by *leaders* and the implementation as being completed by *managers*. I mostly agree, but I also feel that effective leaders have to help out in the implementation. Even if it is just to set an example, it's imperative that leaders develop a can-do and proactive mindset and make things happen around them. As Will Rogers reminds us, "Even if you are on the right track, you'll get run over if you just sit there." Procrastination is living in yesterday, avoiding what you have to do today, and therefore inevitably failing tomorrow. The shortest answer to getting things done and being successful is usually doing.

Your world has an infinite number of possible futures. The decisions—and more importantly, the actions—you make today decide the kind of world you will experience tomorrow. **But you need to get into the habit of making decisions!** Let's use a maze analogy to illustrate. Imagine you see in front of you four distinct paths you can take. If you overanalyze and wait to try to figure out the best path, you may become paralyzed by analysis and not do anything.

If you decide to go down one path, the others will fade and this path will light up, revealing to you people, clues, knowledge, and experience that will assist. The point is that these other helpers are only revealed once you make the decision and commit. Otherwise, you will be standing at the beginning of the maze wondering what to do. At the beginning of the maze, do you worry so much about which is the best path that you do nothing? No, of course not!

You try one path and go from there. It may be wrong, but trying something is infinitely better than doing nothing. Doing separates you from the crowd of talkers. Getting in the habit of doing things and taking control will help you move towards worthy goals. As I often tell people, "If you don't vote, then just be quiet and quit complaining about the state of the country."

If you do things, you take control of your life and gain followers who can make larger impacts. A similar analogy is if you are driving across a country. You can only see the small piece of road directly ahead of you. That is really all that you need to make it across the entire country. You don't need to see the total path, but instead have faith that it is there. You will experience many ups and downs, bumps and detours, but you will eventually make it all the way across. You just have to be committed. Martina Navratilova, the great tennis player, said it best when she stated, "The difference between involvement and commitment is like ham and eggs. The chicken is involved; the pig is committed."

Successful people make decisions quickly (once they have as much information as they can get) and change their minds, if at all, slowly. Unsuccessful people make decisions very slowly, and then change them quickly and frequently. When you want celebrated results, you must introduce an element of urgency to the process. **One** of these days will often turn into **none** of these days. Consider also what you can cut out of your life to make way for better things. The starting point of making better decisions is to stop making worse decisions. The best remedy for being overwhelmed is action. Don't complain about things; it is better to light a candle than complain about the darkness.

So where should you focus your efforts? Leaders realize the value of spending as much time as possible on things that are important but not urgent. These people are by far the most productive. The following matrix is adapted from Stephen Covey's wonderful classic on leadership, *The 7 Habits of Highly Effective People*. This tool will help you prioritize tasks based on their impact on your long-term goals and values. By understanding the difference between "important" and "urgent," you can become more efficient, reduce unnecessary stress, and achieve a better work-life balance.

	URGENT	NOT URGENT
IMPORTANT	1	2
NOT IMPORTANT	3	4

According to the above 2x2 matrix:

1 = URGENT and IMPORTANT—Emergency situations that require immediate attention, such as firefighting. Note, some people's jobs are mostly rooted in this section, such as firefighter, air traffic controllers, traders, and so on. This does not mean that folks in these roles cannot become leaders, but more so that this tool cannot be accurately used to help prioritize since the priorities for those professions are nearly all both urgent and important.

2 = **NOT URGENT and IMPORTANT**—Things that you should do, but don't have to do right now. **This is where you want to spend most of your time**. If you spend lots of time here, there will be fewer things that move into quadrant 1. Take exercise as an example. It is important, but not urgent. You do not need to run around your location right now, but you do need to do some exercise at some point. If you don't exercise at all, your health may move to quadrant 1 and become both urgent and important. The same goes for relationship building. You don't need to build your relationships right at this moment, but you do need to eventually; otherwise, your relationship issues may move to quadrant 1 and become urgent and important. You will also become incredibly more efficient and productive, and far less prone to procrastination, if you focus on this quadrant.

3 = **URGENT and NOT IMPORTANT**—Think carefully about meeting the urgency for these unimportant things, like interruptions or phone calls—do they add value?

4 = **NOT URGENT and NOT IMPORTANT**—This includes time-wasters such as TV. You will need some time in this quadrant to relax.

ENCOURAGE OTHERS

"Flatter me, and I may not believe you.
Criticize me, and I may not like you.
Ignore me, and I may not forgive you.
Encourage me, and I will not forget you."

—WILLIAM ARTHUR WARD

To be an effective leader, you have to develop others. Even if you are remarkably talented, you will realize very quickly that there is only so much you can achieve by yourself. Great leaders surround themselves with outstanding talent and empower them enough to shine. How do you get the best out of others? If you hand-hold or micromanage them, then you are doing some of the work. You want people around you to demonstrate their full potential because of the way you encourage them. The encouragement can come in many forms, for example, verbal affirmations, rewards, incentives, and so on. If you set them free, validate their efforts and make them feel good, they will surprise you with just how much they can do. Spend your life lifting people up, not putting people down.

You want to show others that you understand them. If they can see that you truly get what they are going through, they are far more likely to follow you. Practicing Golden Rule behaviour (treating others like you would want to be treated) goes a long way.

Bob Marley spoke these immortal words: “You can fool some people sometimes, but you can’t fool all the people all the time.” In our context, this means leaders can mask their deficiencies with bluster and smiles and charisma to a point, but eventually, their lack of substance and empathy will shine through. (As a slightly cheeky retort, George W. Bush also stated in jest that “You can fool some of the people all the time, and those are the ones you want to concentrate on.”)

Things sometimes go wrong, and a good mantra to keep in mind is “praise in public and criticize in private.” When things have gone well or people have excelled, then let others know who specifically was instrumental. Name names, and describe why these people were so effective. Don’t just take credit yourself, but rather acknowledge the efforts of others, even if you did most of the work. Why? Not only does this practice motivate your people to do more in the future, but it is likely that everyone listening already knows how instrumental you were. You are the leader in this situation—it is obvious that you were likely heavily involved.

When there is criticism to be communicated, **do not do so in front of others**. There is a reason that most customer service representatives are trained to take you away into another room or private area. When there are others watching, embarrassment can increase exponentially, and indeed we usually behave differently knowing that others are there. What are you really trying to achieve? Do you wish to embarrass or hurt someone, or do you want them to learn and not repeat the mistake again?

If it's the second option, then criticize them in private. The first option will more likely lead to resentment and, ironically, will embarrass you as an immature leader who does not understand communication or motivation.

When your team is going through hard times, you can remind them that the pain now is temporary, whereas the accomplishments later will be totally worth it. In this instance, I love H. G. Wells's quote to remind us of the fleeting nature of anguish: "The crisis of today is the joke of tomorrow." You can also comfort people by saying, "Don't worry, in three-months' time we will be looking back at this and laughing!" That may not come to pass (you may be crying after six months!), but it is the positive attitude that is infectious and will help move things forward.

Encouraging others to drive for success involves igniting their passion. As William Hazlitt said, "A strong passion for any object will ensure success, for the desire of the end will point out the means." Confucius told us many years ago to "Choose a job you love, and you will never have to work a day in your life." This is true for you individually and also points out how a deep passion and desire from those around you will make them go over and above what is required. (On this note of doing what you love, I like to modify the traditional wisdom a little. In my mind, **as long as about 80 to 90 percent of what you do is what you love, you will be OK**. For example, there are some parts of my job (marking, dealing with difficult students, some administration, etc.) that I do not particularly enjoy. However, the vast majority of my job (preparing and teaching classes) brings me a deep sense of joy and satisfaction, and so I am happy.

GO BEYOND (FOR THE FUTURE LEADERS)

"We all die. The goal isn't to live forever. The goal is to create something that will."

—CHUCK PALAHNIUK

Anything other than the relentless pursuit of excellence leads to the complacent acceptance of the mediocre. **Every great achievement was once considered impossible.** Who really succeeds in life? It's the people who go above and beyond. I heard the saying "Bite off more than you can chew, and then chew like hell" (Peter Brock) early in my teenage years, and it stuck with me for inspiration. Successful leaders are extremely busy, but they somehow manage to balance everything and get all of their key tasks done. I believe it's largely because they have so much energy, since they believe wholly in whatever it is they are doing. Even things that seem daunting and initially impossible (such as balancing completing a degree while working full time and raising a family) can be completed if you take it one step at a time and develop time management skills to help you through.

I marvel at some of my professional MBA students who have to perform this exact balance. There is very little wasted time, and they become extraordinarily efficient in group meetings and with completing assignments and making the most out of every extremely busy day. Whatever you believe your limits are, know that you can likely do more. I am not saying that you should continually do more (your chances of burnout will increase), but just have faith that our bodies and minds can put up with way more than most people can imagine.

The opposite of success is not failure, but settling for mediocrity. Going beyond means doing what other people don't want to do or don't feel is necessary. Allow me to explain by using the example of informational interviews. If you have not heard of them, they are fantastic ways to showcase your skills to a prospective employer. Informational interviews are an informal conversation with a person working for a company or in an industry that interests you. In effect, you are interviewing someone from a company to find out more about the field. Informational interviews can also be seen as a way for you to highlight your skills and demonstrate why you would be a great employee to hire. If you wish to take this path, there is a very effective technique, which goes far beyond what the average person will do, that I recommend to all the students I mentor.

The way to look at informational interviews is from both sides of the table. On one side, you are interviewing someone from the organization to find out more about roles, challenges, and what it is generally like to work there. On the other side, you also have a company representative who could potentially open all sorts of doors for you. Much like an internship or co-op placement, it's an opportunity for you to learn about each other.

In my mind, an average informational interview is strictly one-way. You ask the company representative questions, and they respond the best they can. A better informational interview is when it's more of a conversation, and you can subtly introduce your various skills and unique background to the other side. In an average informational interview, the other side will feel they have answered your questions, and everyone can move on. With a great informational interview, the other side will likely think, *Wait a minute, maybe we should be exploring hiring such a talent!*

So the question becomes: How do you make a fantastic impression? Researching the company/industry well and having a solid set of interesting, probing, and enlightening questions is just a start. You want to go further by weaving in your own key attributes to the questions and conversation. For example, you may preface a question about the culture of the organization by stating how you have learned, the painful way, how to work in diverse teams through lots of experience in school. Maybe you will briefly mention the hardest lesson you have learned, and then go on to ask if these problems persist in the organization. That is much better than simply asking, "What is it like to work here?"

Of course, your goal is to highlight your key accomplishments (not in a boastful way, but rather as feeder points to your questions), but you don't want to make it all about you. The key to avoiding that is to think of subtle questions. My favorite questions are nonstandard ones that force the other person to stop and think. You can guarantee that they have heard all the standard questions before, but reframing them will likely cause the other person to remember you, because they consciously had to consider your question. For the standard questions, they will likely be on autopilot with their response.

The absolutely essential piece to informational interviews is what happens *afterwards*. Most people simply follow up by writing a highly effusive message along the lines of, "Thank you so very much for your incredible wisdom and the time you spent with me ... Blah,

blah, blah." That is OK for an average person. However, to stick out, you need to go much further. My advice is to have one of your questions during the interview be something like, "What are the three things that keep you awake at night?" or "What are the three biggest challenges facing you today?" (Even better is to preface this by saying you believe the three biggest issues of their industry are X, Y, and Z, and asking, "Is that accurate?") Then, in your follow-up email, you thank them and go on to say you have been thinking about the major issues and have come up with a one-pager for some high-level ideas.

You won't be able to solve all of their problems, but you can certainly provide ideas (say, three bullet points for each issue). For example, most organizations have problems with recruitment, so one of your bullet points may be to concentrate efforts on various postsecondary institutions who graduate folks with the right skill sets. **The point is to demonstrate skills the organization is looking for**, and by doing this one-pager, you are demonstrating initiative, discipline, knowledge of the company and industry, creativity, effective communication, critical thinking, analytical skills, problem-solving, awareness, etc.—all vital skills for almost any employee. Even better is including some research that will help back up your recommendations. You finish the email by saying how you would love to discuss further or go into more depth with recommendations.

You won't be able to go into this much depth for lots of organizations, so choose wisely who you think is worth making the considerable time and effort for. They may not have a position for you now, but in the future, if something does become available, they will likely contact you first. Why? **Because you have already demonstrated the skills they're looking for, and there is no need to find others who have those skills.**

STAYING HUMBLE

> *"Being powerful is like being a lady. If you have to tell people you are, then you aren't."*
>
> **—MARGARET THATCHER**

Leadership is seldom *given*. It is *earned* by those who are willing to manifest the boldness and passion that the times require. No matter how successful you are, you want to cultivate character others will want to listen to and follow. It is nice to be important, but extremely more important to be nice. When you are really good at something, there is no need to tell anyone. Your actions will speak more than your words ever could. **Make a lot of mistakes and learn from them**. It is better to err than to not try, for without wrongs there are no rights. People are never jealous of losers. Therefore, if people are jealous of you, you must be doing something right. Just try not to be arrogant about it.

Try to treat people the same. You can tell the truly ***big*** people by the way they treat the supposed ***little*** people. I always make it a point to talk to cleaners, security guards, secretaries,* and all levels of employees with the same enthusiasm and effort as I would senior people. To me, it doesn't matter what your status or job title is. We are all God's children, so just be consistent.

Give others the respect of listening to them, but don't take everything you hear to heart. For example, when I worked in finance, I would often hear from senior folks about the importance of having

---

* Note, I am not saying that cleaners, security guards, and secretaries are little people, but rather, these people are often *seen* and *treated* as less significant in many organizations. In reality, we need many different skills within an organization for it to thrive, and everyone working around you is contributing to the overall direction and atmosphere that you experience.

work-life balance. But on further probing, when I asked them, "How did you get to where you are today?" they informed me that they worked like crazy and had no life! Mark Twain also provides sage advice on dealing with some folks: "Never argue with an idiot. They will drag you down to their level and beat you with experience."

As I said at the beginning of this chapter: Don't measure leadership simply by how successful you are in a given area. Rather, **measure it by how much you contribute back to the society and community that has allowed you to become a leader**. Be yourself always—everyone else is already taken! How you frame challenges will also determine how you overcome them. I love Jim Rohn's quote, which hammers this point home: "Don't wish it was easier, wish you were better. Don't wish for less problems, wish for more skills. Don't wish for less challenge, wish for more wisdom." This advice helps turn your attitude into a more positive and empowered one, rather than defeatist. The situations do not change, but you do.

DON'T	DO
WISH IT WAS EASIER	WISH YOU WERE BETTER
WISH FOR FEWER PROBLEMS	WISH FOR MORE SKILLS
WISH FOR FEWER CHALLENGES	WISH FOR MORE WISDOM

Paul Romer, a Stanford economist, coined the phrase "A crisis is a terrible thing to waste." This refers to how every cloud has a silver lining, and you can learn from any situation, good or bad. I also believe it refers to how people typically reveal themselves under pressure. Under normal circumstances, I may be extremely polite and cordial to those around me, opening doors and letting others go first. However, if the fire alarm goes off, I may just knock you all out of the way to get to the exit first! (I wouldn't by the way, but you get the point.) Under pressure, people reveal their true colors. Make sure your true colors are worth revealing!

Leadership can be terribly lonely and intensely frustrating. You may get criticism for failing when you were expecting praise for trying. That's OK—remember to stay positive at all times, and your time will come. A story to illustrate this point: I remember one summer when I was leaving for work and saw that my front lawn was covered with leaves, twigs, and all kinds of debris. Knowing that my kids get bored pretty quickly during the holidays, I called my daughter when she woke up and tasked her to have the front lawn clear by the time I returned that evening.

After a long day at work, I drove back along my street expecting (or hoping!) to see a nice, clean front lawn. To my horror, the front lawn looked the same, if not worse, than in the morning! I was not happy with my daughter and proceeded inside to ask why the work was not done.

"You had all day to do one thing, and it looks like you have not even started. Why did you not clean the lawn?" I asked in a slightly upset tone. I was criticizing my daughter for failing. Her reply surprised me. I was half expecting her to offer excuses, but instead she went on to describe how she had actually tried many things. She had tried some of our tools (rakes and hoes) but found them too difficult and large, so she borrowed some from a neighbor. Some of these tools needed cleaning, and she got them ready. There was no room in our garbage bins, so she emptied them all to get ready. She had even researched the best way to clean the different parts of the lawn (edging, flower beds, grass, etc.). She had done a lot, but I just couldn't *see* any results.

As she spoke, it reminded me of the painting profession. Most of the difficult and hard work when painting is in the preparation and the cleanup. The actual painting is usually very straightforward and quick. But as an observer, we simply look to see if the wall is painted to signify success. In my example, I was simply seeing if the lawn was clear, disregarding all of the prep needed and the fact that my daughter had completed around 70 percent of the task.

The point is I had criticized her for failing, but she was expecting praise for trying. This taught me a great lesson—always find out as many details as possible before making a comment! My daughter taught me another lesson that day. She could have easily responded to my gruffness and irritable opening criticism by getting upset, angry, or somehow escalating the situation. Instead, she calmly explained all of the things she had done, and waited for me to reassess her perceived laziness.

Two huge skills that need to be developed are being *brave* and being *adaptable*. If you are not brave and always take the safe option, then so much in the world will be beyond your reach. Minimizing risk is advised, but it's hard to completely eliminate risk. Being brave requires a leap in faith as you will be going into uncharted territory with relatively little certainty. Going into a situation with no certain outcome requires bravery and the ability to tolerate change, or to be adaptable. These twin skills will give you the confidence to explore and experiment, having faith and knowing in the back of your mind that you can succeed, even if you don't necessarily know exactly how things will pan out.

I love the following quote from David Lloyd George: "Don't be afraid to take a big step if one is indicated. You can't cross a chasm in two small jumps." What a wonderful analogy for being brave and taking a calculated chance. If you are only willing to take the easy path, then life will be hard. But if you are willing to do what is challenging and what will push you further, then life will be easy.

On the topic of bravery, courageous people get just as nervous as everyone else. If you have a major speech to give, and you look at others and think that they seem more confident than you, you are likely wrong. It's not that they don't get anxious, it's just that they believe **their message is more important than their nerves**. If you are getting butterflies in your stomach, don't believe that you shouldn't be feeling them. It is completely natural to feel apprehensive. Just return your focus to what is important, and the nerves will take care of themselves. Even though I have delivered thousands of classes, I still get a little nervous before each one. You just never know what may happen. To get over the nerves, I simply believe that the lessons I teach are **far more important** than my butterflies. The butterflies are fleeting, but the messages may change lives.

Being brave and adaptable will come in handy if there is ever any downturn in your fortunes. Be prepared, for it is when the tide goes out that you will see who is naked. As Mike Tyson put it, "Everybody has a plan until they get punched in the mouth!" Take risks, for most people chart a path so that they can achieve a safe way to death! Charles Darwin put it well when he said, "It is not the strongest species that survive, nor the most intelligent that survives. It is the one that is most adaptable to change." Be strong in your will but also flexible when needed. Stay humble. Consider the following:

> *"Achieve Results, But never glory in them.*
> *Achieve Results, But never boast.*
> *Achieve Results, But never be proud.*
> *Achieve Results, Because this is the natural way.*
> *Achieve Results, But not through violence."*
>
> **—LAO TZU, TAO TE CHING**

The great fallacy is that those at the top of any organization have thought through all of the possibilities and implications and that actions taken have been carefully thought through and scrutinized. In reality, those at the top are invariably so busy that there is no time to think through everything, let alone come up with many new ideas. Therefore, some of the most valuable people in any organization are those who come up with new ideas and follow through with implementation. Become one of those people, and you can be a leader.

My biggest pet peeve is arrogance. Anyone who thinks they are better than anyone else because they are smarter, richer, or ahead on any dimension is, in my opinion, deluded. We are all God's children and all deserve respect for who we are. Be careful not to display arrogance; it can be both direct and indirect. Looking down on people who don't have what you have is obviously arrogant. However, if you believe that people "should" do this or understand that, and if you get upset at them for not doing so, then you may be indirectly displaying arrogance, as you are expecting them to have the same intellect or understanding as you do.

For example, if you are in a slow-moving line at a grocery store where the store employee seems to be taking forever to serve customers, and you are getting frustrated at them for doing so, maybe you are being indirectly arrogant. You are assuming that they have the ability, presence, and motivation to do the job more quickly, but in reality, they may not. Or maybe they are just having the worst day of their life. Take a moment to assess the situation, and watch out for indirect arrogance.

ARROGANCE	INDIRECT ARROGANCE
Thinking you are better than someone because you are smarter, richer, or ahead on any dimension	Assuming that someone has the ability, presence, or motivation to do something better or faster

---

Be careful of office politics, which can be defined as building and using power of some sort to get things done. Note, not all office politics are negative. Some can be positive. For example, if you spend the first three weeks at a new workplace taking all of the senior folks out for lunch or a coffee, this can be seen as playing politics. You are building relationships not only to help you in the future but also to ensure favouritism. There is nothing wrong with doing this, and indeed the practice is smiled upon by many mentors. However, if you use your relationships to unfairly secure advantages over those more deserving, then politics can be seen as negative. Likewise, if you talk nicely about people in front of some folks but rubbish about them behind their backs to fit in or appeal to certain people, you are playing politics in a negative way. (Remember, someone has to get behind you before they stab you in the back!)

If you want to be a leader in the future, I wholly recommend that you never criticize your boss. Even if they are clearly one of the worst leaders ever and a laughing stock among your colleagues, do not speak poorly of them. Why is this important? If they are indeed incompetent, then others will notice, and your words will not make any difference. However, when they are fired or reassigned (or they move on willingly), those who heard your criticism will remember what you said, and your loyalty may be called into question. You may think that you were simply voicing what everyone else was saying, but you have inadvertently damaged your own reputation. Of course, if you are asked for feedback by someone more senior, then you can use your discretion to respond in a diplomatic manner. Just don't get dragged down into the circles that criticize and mock other people.

You do not need to play the game, but you have to be aware that a game is being played. In my experience, there are some employees who do not want to play politics. They want to come to work, do a good job, and not worry about artificially making themselves look better. However, from what I see, if you ignore the game, you are likely to be run over by the game. You do not need to actively contribute to office politics, but you have to be aware that the political games will be played. And simply ignoring them will not make you immune to other people's actions. Consider the following:

> *"The best soldier does not attack.*
> *The superior fighter succeeds without violence.*
> *The greatest conqueror wins without a struggle.*
> *The most successful manager leads*
> *without dictating.*
> *This is intelligent non aggressiveness."*
>
> **—LAO TZU, TAO TE CHING**

What should you do when you become a successful leader? Don't let up, and don't get complacent. Bad habits are like a comfortable bed—easy to get into, but hard to get out of. Well, you can take things even further and use those leadership skills (such as braveness, awareness, adaptability, and humility) that you have learned along the way to make a difference elsewhere.

There are many leaders out there in their own fields, people who excel and are admired by their peers. But to be a true leader, you have to become a leader in more than one field. How? For example, you could excel in more than one area of life, such as excelling in your professional field while also being a kind member of the community, forsaking many income opportunities to instead donate your time and money to good causes. You could be outstanding in your business field and run an amazing household. True leaders make time to excel in more than one area of life.

How do you know if you are a successful leader? I like to use an example of someone whom I admire tremendously, someone you probably have never heard of. Growing up watching football in England, Paul McGrath was one of the best defenders I have ever seen. Even though he played for my favorite team's archrivals, his anticipation and ability to snuff out other attacks were remarkable. As a defender myself, I marveled at how he always seemed to be in the right place at the right time.

It was only later that I discovered just how challenging a life Paul had experienced. He spent most of his childhood in foster care, suffered a catastrophic mental breakdown for almost a year at the age of twenty, where he remained in a "trance-like state, unspeaking, incontinent, and covered in bedsores,* endured alcoholism (including during his career), couldn't train because of injuries (including eight surgeries on his knee), and attempted suicide at least four times. Learning about his history elevated him even further in my mind, for he overcame such adversity to become one of the best

* McGrath, Paul. *Back from the Brink*. Arrow Books, 2007.

players that I have ever seen. He retired a long time ago, and he still contributes back to society and has five grandchildren.

I believe Paul's story offers nice clues on how to be a leader. He impressed me very specifically in three layers:

- **Layer 1**—Paul was outstanding (one of the best in the world) at what he did, and this can be confirmed by many sources.
- **Layer 2**—He achieved so much despite having major issues off the field with vicious alcoholism, mental disease, and a body that disallowed training. (He was only allowed to play games—imagine what he could have been like if he could train!)
- **Layer 3**—So many testimonials from people who have met him over the years, praising his patience, calmness, and aura. By all accounts he is an extremely classy guy.[†]

† Ibid.

One point to note is that it's Layer 1, being superb in your field, upon which all of your other success in leadership is built. Layers 2 and 3 would not happen (or would be vastly less significant) without a strong Layer 1.

As an aside, I love to probe when I am interviewing people on something that the candidate is outstanding in. It does not matter if their examples are in academics, work, sports, a musical instrument, etc. **What matters is that they are outstanding in something.** Why? Because when you are outstanding at one thing, you can usually be outstanding in many things. You have learned many key skills, such as discipline, work ethic, persistence, and dealing with disappointment, which indicate to me that you can be outstanding at whatever position I am interviewing you for.

I would like to finish this chapter with a saying that I have framed and hung up in my office. This is something I see every single day, and it reminds me of specific points to look for to measure success:

To Laugh Often and Much

"To laugh often and much;
to win the respect of the intelligent people
and the affection of children;
to earn the appreciation of honest critics
and endure the betrayal of false friends;
to appreciate the beauty;
to find the best in others;
to leave the world a bit better
whether by a healthy child, a garden patch,

or a redeemed social condition;
to know one life has breathed easier
because you lived here.
This is to have succeeded."

—RALPH WALDO EMERSON

SUMMARY AND KEY LEARNING POINTS

- Leadership is the ability to influence others to achieve goals, and you can measure Leadership by the number of admiring followers you have and your ability to excel in your field.
- The most important attribute to develop for Leadership is **integrity**. This is followed closely by self-awareness, humility, bravery, resilience, adaptability, and being action-orientated.
- Major accomplishments will take time and will include many failures that you, as a leader, will need to get used to.
- Leaders have four main responsibilities: provide direction, take action, encourage others, and go beyond.
- Keep messaging succinct.
- Spend a little extra time at the beginning to make sure you involve people's hearts and foster commitment.
- You need both *ideas* and *implementation* to be a successful leader.
- Praise in public and criticize in private.

- Encourage others by igniting their passion.
- Give people the respect that they all deserve.
- Consider how much you can give back to the society and community that has allowed you to become a leader.
- During a crisis or critical event, people (and organizations) will reveal themselves.
- To become a stronger leader, you must become braver and more adaptable.
- Office politics can be challenging and derailing, and even though you may choose not to contribute, you must be aware that games are being played.
- If you become a strong leader, use your skills to lead in more than one field. The world needs more real leaders.
- True leaders excel in their own field, overcome adversity, and stay humble.

Exercises

FINDING YOUR WHY

Most of us know what it is that we or others do. Some of us know how we or others do it. But very few people know **why**. You want to build the habit of getting to the fundamental why of everything around us. By doing so, priorities will become clear and your comfort in defining a purpose will increase exponentially.

As an example, when you ask most people "*Why* do you work?" the common response is, "To earn money." Push yourself by continually asking why until you cannot go any further.

“**Why** do you work?”
“To earn money.”

“Why?”
“To save up and spend.”

“Why?”
“So that I can cover all expenses and feel confident that I have enough.”

“Why?”
“So that I can do all the things I want to do in life.”

“Why?”
“So that I feel secure and am making the most of my life.”

“Why?”
“That security and confidence will make me happy.”

The secret is to keep going until you can go no further. At the end (and along the way), you will discover the true purposes behind why you do what you do. Getting in the habit of thinking this way will make it much easier for you to craft messages that resonate and motivate those around you.

In the following table, answer the questions by continually asking why until you can go no further. Write down all of the answers in your journey.

INITIAL QUESTION	KEEP GOING BY ASKING WHY QUESTIONS UNTIL YOU CAN ASK NO MORE.
Why do you work or go to school?	
Why do you want to be a leader?	
Why is leadership important to you?	
Why do you want to make a difference?	
Why do you want to be successful?	
Why do you want to travel?	
Why do you want to celebrate achievement?	
Why do you want to be a good parent or sibling or child or partner?	

WHERE YOU SPEND YOUR TIME

We are typically highly reactive beings. Something happens, and we need to respond. True leaders will deploy an alternative approach where they will seek to be proactive and deal with issues before they arise. The starting point is to become more aware of how you are spending your time. This exercise will raise your awareness and will provide insights on whether you are making the most of the time available to you.

Using Stephen Covey's adapted matrix below, keep a journal of approximately how much time you spend in each quadrant every day over the next week.

	URGENT	NOT URGENT
IMPORTANT	1	2
NOT IMPORTANT	3	4

1= **Urgent and Important**—Emergency situations that require immediate attention, such as firefighting.

2= **Not Urgent and Important**—Things that you should do but don't have to do right now. **This is where you want to spend most of your time**. If you spend lots of time here, there will be fewer things in quadrant 1. You will also become exceedingly more efficient and productive and far less prone to procrastination.

3= **Urgent and Not Important**—Think carefully about meeting the urgency for these unimportant things, like interruptions or phone calls—do they add value?

4= **Not Urgent and Not Important**—Time-wasters such as TV. You will need some of these to relax.

- What is important to do in your life but is not urgent? You can think of health, wealth, relationships, work, school, and so on. Can you immediately commit to completing some of these important tasks?
- How can you restructure your time or life to spend more time in quadrant 2?

LAYERS OF LEADERSHIP

The three layers of leadership dictate that true leaders excel in their own field, overcome adversity, and stay humble. The purpose of this exercise is to assess your current leadership level according to the three layers in order to build self-awareness and to identify gaps to close in your leadership journey.

- Think of all areas where you can consider yourself a leader. Do not be shy—you do not have to have a fancy title and it does not have to be something universally admired, but rather, something that you simply excel in (and we can define "excel" by something that you are better than, say, 80 percent of the general public or those who are in the field itself at).
- Examples can include a specific aspect of your work, an academic subject or topic, a sport, a musical instrument, a hobby or pastime, a skill or

behavioural trait, a type of test or task, and so on.

- The areas identified will be your Layer 1 traits (you excel in them).
- Fill out the following table to ascertain Layers 2 and 3. Try to come up with as many pieces of adversity that you have overcome to achieve excellence (Layer 2) and as many pieces of evidence that prove you are staying grounded and humble in light of your excellence (Layer 3).

LAYER 1 Leadership areas	**LAYER 2** Adversities that you have overcome	**LAYER 3** Proof that you are staying humble

Most people find that Layer 2 (Adversity) is fairly simple to complete (and can also be eye-opening). Layer 3 is usually the tricky one, though. Is there any evidence that you stay humble?

Have you showed off in the past? Do you help others, patiently, who are not at your level? Do you realize that there are people even better than you and that you have a lot to learn? These questions are interesting to consider, and thoughtful review may provide valuable insights on becoming a stronger leader.

Reflection Questions

- Who are the leaders that you admire most in life, either present or past? What is it about these leaders, specifically, that you admire?
- What have you been procrastinating on? Why? Can you take immediate action to move you closer to what you want?
- Do you treat all people alike? If not, why not?
- What do you get nervous about? For each item, can you think about and list what is far more important than the nerves that you feel?
- Which arenas would you like to become a leader in? Why? What's your plan to become a leader in that arena?
- How easy do you find it to motivate others?

CHAPTER 9

CONCLUSION

"Life is what happens to you while you are busy making other plans."

—ALLEN SAUNDERS

After reading this book, I hope you have been challenged to look at the world differently. We have scratched the surface of vast, important topics, where improvements in any one area will have a substantial effect on all of the other areas, as well as your overall happiness and attitude.

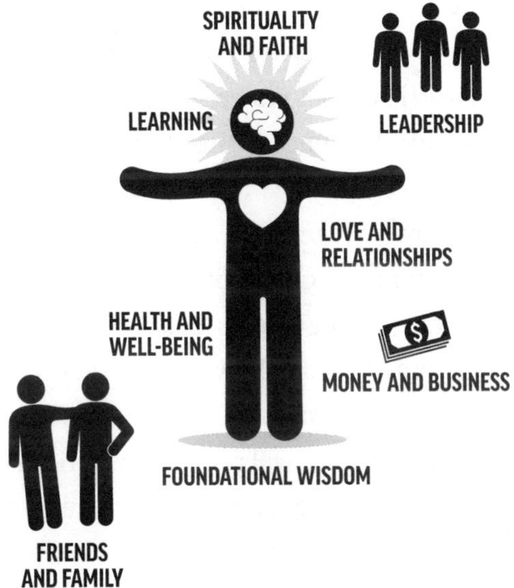

In the end, life is really like a river that has many unexpected turns but ultimately ends up in the great ocean, where you will connect with everyone else. **The more you wish life (in general) was different, the more you are fighting nature**, and life will seem stressful and difficult. Go with the flow and try to be happy, content, and confident that your life is transpiring exactly how it should. Everything happens for a reason—it may not be clear at the time, but have patience.

Your newfound knowledge on wisdom should help you in multiple scenarios. Your ways of thinking about and framing situations should help you remain more positive and confident towards challenges and deal better with setbacks, as you understand the bigger picture. I have found that having a deeper sense of wisdom on any topic helps me see that topic from multiple perspectives. You will find yourself going down paths (both physical and mental) that you previously never dreamed about. And of course, it was all meant to help you with your journey.

Time also takes on a different meaning, because wise people tend to be more present and spend less time worrying about the past or future. As Dale Carnegie so eloquently put it: "Today is the tomorrow you worried about yesterday." (Another, similar quote I really like comes from Laurence J. Peter: "An economist is an expert who will know tomorrow why the things he predicted yesterday didn't happen today.") We tend to remember the past with a fond filter, because we forget about all of the stress and problems we faced to achieve things. Most parents look back fondly at when their kids were small, forgetting just how drained they felt at the time.

As you grow wiser, you will notice a rise in your decision-making ability. Things will pop into your head (such as the right question to ask or the right perspective to frame a situation in a helpful light) more often and with more support. Everything from short-term decisions (for example, checking for toilet paper before sitting down) to longer-term decisions (such as deciding on a career or where you want to live) will seem simpler and less stressful. The increased positivity will permeate your entire life, and you will, for example, be able to use your wit to amuse rather than abuse others.

Soon, you will be startled at the number of opportunities coming your way. Why does this occur? Well, firstly, you have created a wise mindset that is more likely to notice opportunities around you. **Your different perspectives towards life will also open different doors with people and situations**. As a wiser person, you will attract more attention from others who sense change and maturity in you. And once these opportunities present themselves, you will have the wisdom and knowledge to make the best use of them. **You will feel luckier**. As Tony Robbins (someone whom I admire as one of the best communicators of our time) reminds us, "The meeting of preparation with opportunity generates the offspring we call luck."

When stepping back from thinking about an issue, remember to stop and occasionally smell the roses. **Don't overlook life's small joys when searching for the big ones**. How do you do this? By fostering a sense of gratitude and making this attitude towards gratitude central to your life.

NEXT STEPS

> *"Never look down to test the ground before taking your next step; only he who keeps his eye fixed on the far horizon will find the right road."*
>
> **—DAG HAMMARSKJÖLD**

So what to do now? The first thing is to make sure that you have read all the chapters in this book and have done your best to complete the exercises at the end of each chapter. If you merely skimmed the exercises or tried them superficially, then now is the time to go back and give each of them your entire attention. **The exercises will help integrate the material into your being and, more importantly, personalize the lessons to you and your life.**

I do not want this to be another book that you read, find some useful pieces, and forget about quickly. To really internalize the material (assuming you are not already incredibly wise), you need to actively take things further. Why not set yourself a challenge? (Challenges help by stimulating your competitive nature and by using the magic of goals.)

You do not have to do everything in this book immediately, but try the following. Make a list of at least ten practices that have resonated with you while reading this book. (You can have fewer or more than ten, but aim for about ten.) You must be convinced that incorporating these practices in your day-to-day actions will improve your life in some way.

Then, make a table with the ten practices as the left-most column and the next twenty days as the top-most row. Every day, simply use the table cells as tick-boxes indicating whether or not you completed each practice. (You may have to amend slightly, as you may not be able to complete some of your practices every day). If you can keep up any of the practices for twenty days, there is a good chance that you have developed the habit to the point of not needing daily checklists.

If your life improves in any way, you can repeat this exercise with more difficult practices. The point is that you are **actively engaged in using the wisdom from this book to improve your**

life. Even more importantly, you will have started the journey to internalizing and spreading more wisdom. The time to do this is right now. Not tomorrow, not next week, not January 1, but right now. **One of the greatest enemies to success in life is the belief that we have plenty of time**. If you are the type of person who constantly puts things off and believes they will all magically occur in the future, then you need to change. Right now. Commit now to even one change, and you will have made progress.

You never know what is going to happen next in your life. Tomorrow could bring joy, or it could bring despair. All you can do is be strong—mentally, physically, emotionally, and spiritually—and then you can best deal with anything that comes your way. Concentrate on getting strong in every way as much as you can, and not at the expense of others. Concentrate on building your wisdom to help smooth your path.

The final two exercises at the end of this chapter will help you develop written goals and visualize the fantastic future that you deserve.

There are many helpful resources that go far deeper into the material covered in this book. At the end, I have included a bibliography of books that have resonated deeply with me and have helped feed my wisdom. Take your pick from the topics that interest you, and cultivate a learning and curiosity mindset to delve deeper. I invite you to visit my website at perryatwal.com, where you will find lots more information and resources to help in your path.

REFLECTION EXERCISES

Instead of having a summary, exercises, and reflection questions at the end of this concluding chapter (as we have had for all previous chapters), I wanted to leave you with two powerful reflection exercises that will help provide direction and accountability for your spiritual path.

WRITTEN GOALS EXERCISE

The importance of having goals has been discussed elsewhere in this book, and hopefully it is clear to you that without goals, without knowing where you are going, it is harder to motivate yourself and build confidence. **Goals provide clarity by providing a light for your future,** and they help measure how far you have come and have left to go. Let us take this a little further now, and concentrate on having *written* goals.

A growing body of research indicates writing down goals increases your chances of achieving them by 35 to 42 percent. That is significant. Having written goals separates you from the vast majority of people. We can all dream about possible futures, but when you write down your goals, you create a sense of accountability for yourself. You will have a tangible reminder of what is important to you and where you are headed, which will result in increased levels of motivation. Written goals engage both the cognitive and emotional parts of the brain, resulting in higher chances of success.

Writing your goals down also helps turn that swirl in your head (fuzzy views of the future) into clear, measurable targets that will aid your decision-making and provide direction when you are stuck. You cannot just write down random thoughts and expect to be successful, so the process of goal writing will turn those random thoughts into concrete, logical targets, and just as important, provide a filter to assess new opportunities that come your way.

How to write down your goals:

- Consider the main areas of your life. You can use any framework, and the chapter headings in this book give one way to organize them (Love and Relationships, Friends and Family, Health and Well-Being, Learning, Money and Business, Spirituality and Faith, Leadership).
- For each area, consider two or three positive goals that would, if attained, mean fantastic success within the area *for you*. Note, some people like to split up their goals into short- (say, achievable within the next year) and long-term timeframes. You want to push yourself (you might as well aim high) but also be reasonable. (For example, if you set a goal of being able to run around the world in thirty seconds, you *will* be disappointed.)
- To simplify, make sure you have no more than three goals within each area and no more than eighteen overall. From my experience, having too many tends to dilute your goals, your focus, and your energy.
- Make sure your goals are measurable and have associated timeframes. Otherwise, how will you know if you meet your goals or when you are supposed to achieve them?

    - For example, goals of "losing weight" or "making lots of money" are too vague.
    - Replace those with goals such as "weighing XXX pounds on Jan 1, 20YY" and "earning $YYY per year by the year 20ZZ."

- Also, ensure your goals are within your control. Having a goal of your favorite sports team winning the World Championship is worthless unless you are actively participating to make it happen.
- Once you have your goals edited to where you want them, take out a pen and write them as neatly as you can (with a pen, *do not type*) on a blank piece of paper.*
- Put this piece of paper somewhere you can easily access and, therefore, review to keep up the motivation.

My family repeats the above exercise every January 1 (most long-term goals stay the same, but the yearly goals obviously change), and together we write our individual goals as well as our family goals (each one of us writes the family goals).

I am not a big fan of New Year's resolutions, for I believe if you really want to do something, the time is right now or today, rather than waiting for an arbitrary date in the future such as January 1. However, the beginning or end of the year is a great time to reflect on what happened and where you are in achieving your goals, because the calendar year is a simple cycle to follow.

Note, there are many frameworks and websites for helping writing goals. The most common framework is the SMART mnemonic (Specific, Measurable, Achievable, Relevant, and Time-

* One of the most powerful things you can do with any child (say, between the ages of nine and sixteen) is to set aside some time to have them write down their goals. Given the muscles in our hands and wrists are linked to parts of the brain, the act of writing is even more impactful for the younger generations, as they have very strong thumbs (from all the texting and playing games) and strong typing muscles, but relatively weak writing muscles because they simply do not use them as much.

bound). James Clear has also put together a fantastic guide for setting goals at https://jamesclear.com/goal-setting.

VISUALIZATION EXERCISE

Our final exercise is one that, when done properly, will bring you closer to the ideal life you have always wanted. Now that you have written goals, it is time to visualize a fabulous future where your goals have been achieved.

You can visualize several possible situations in the future, and the process is the same for each. I will describe how to do my favorite one, and you can tailor or adapt it for yourself.

- I like to think about a situation that embodies the attainment of as many of my goals as possible. You can be creative here, but I use the example of giving a speech at my retirement party (hopefully, far into the future).
- I like this setting because it allows the embodiment of many of my goals into just one event, namely:

    - Financial, business, and leadership goals (in how I am introduced and the achievements and status that define my career)
    - Friends and family goals (in being surrounded by many of my cherished relationships)
    - Love goals (in my extended tribute to my loving wife)

    - Health and well-being goals (in how I look, feel, and come across)
    - Learning goals (in how I have evolved)
    - Spiritual goals (in my confidence and ability to be in the moment)
    - Your setting can be anything you like, but try to have it encompass as many of your personal goals as possible. Also try to be ambitious—you might as well aim high, given that you can dream anything!
    - Take your time refining your setting to what would make you absolutely ecstatic. You will use this visualization frequently, so it must be something that inspires you.

- Once you have your situation, you can visualize it as often and for as long as you like. A dedicated visualization exercise requires you to be in a quiet place and for you to close your eyes (to avoid distractions). However, I also like visualizing when walking. Having an event to visualize helps, because it focuses my mind on a specific moment, rather than simply feeling wealthy or successful, which can be too broad to concentration on.
- When you wish to visualize, the most important part by far is focusing on the **feeling** the visualization gives you. You should get goose bumps when picturing this fantastic future event. I find that imagining all kinds of details helps the most. For example, for my retirement speech, I may choose to focus on:

- The exact color, brand, and style of my clothing
- The exact color, brand, and style of my wife's and children's clothing
- The exact décor in the room, including the height of the ceiling, the moldings, the color and style of the walls, the type of lighting, etc.;
- The exact nature of the audience, including how many are sitting at each table, their ages, and the applause they regularly break out into
- The words that are used, including those in my own speech, the ones given by the person who introduces me, the mutters of laughter and "Hear, hears" from the audience, what my wife says to me when I sit back down, and so on
- The weather and other time-of-year related details, for example, the flowers blossoming outside in spring
- The smells wafting across the room, including the smell of food and drink, my own cologne, the leather of the furniture, and so on
- The time before and after the event, including the route I take to and from the venue, getting changed and ready in the morning, going for a celebration afterwards, and so on

I appreciate the level of detail above may seem like overkill, but I promise you it is not. The details help elicit the feelings and emotions you are looking for, that is, an almost uncontrollable level of exhilaration because such an amazing future is coming true. Without the details, the visualization will seem vague and fuzzy and more like a pipe dream—unattainable and for someone else. Don't be shy! It is *your* dream!

Consider that visualization has helped everyone from CEOs to athletes to high performers in every field to reach their aspirations. This visualization exercise should be congruent (and not conflicting) with your daily affirmations, and it works wonders when you combine it with those affirmations on your regular walk. Good luck!

Further Reading and Bibliography

In this section, I list the books that have made the biggest impressions on my life, categorized by the main chapters in this book. Being a voracious reader, I like to reread books that have nuggets of wisdom I appreciate, and I have read all of the books here at least twice. The books listed would, in my opinion, be valuable additions to your wisdom library.

CHAPTERS 2 & 3: LOVE AND RELATIONSHIPS AND FRIENDS AND FAMILY

Reaching to Heaven by James Van Praagh

Crucial Confrontations: Tools for Resolving Broken Promises, Violated Expectations, and Bad Behavior by Kerry Patterson, Joseph Grenny, Ron McMillan, and Al Switzler

Overcoming Anger in Your Relationship: How to Break the Cycle of Arguments, Put-Downs, and Stony Silences by W. Robert Nay, PhD

Men Are from Mars, Women Are from Venus by John Gray

Beyond Mars and Venus: Relationship Skills for Today's Complex World by John Gray

Journey of Souls by Michael Newton, PhD

The Charisma Myth: How Anyone Can Master the Art and Science of Personal Magnetism by Olivia Fox Cabane

Coping with Difficult People by Robert Bramson

How to Win Friends and Influence People by Dale Carnegie

How to Do the Work by Nicole LePera

The Art of Seduction by Robert Greene

The 5 Love Languages by Gary Chapman

The Seven Principles for Making Marriage Work by John Gottman and Nan Silver

Everybody Matters: The Extraordinary Power of Caring for Your People Like Family by Bob Chapman and Raj Sisodia

The Conscious Parent: Transforming Ourselves, Empowering Our Children by Shefali Tsabary

The Origins of You by Vienna Pharaon

CHAPTER 4: HEALTH AND WELL-BEING

Outlive: The Science and Art of Longevity by Peter Attia, with Bill Gifford

Breath: The New Science of a Lost Art by James Nestor

Lifespan: Why We Age—and Why We Don't Have To by David Sinclair, with Matthew D. LaPlante

Finding Ultra by Rich Roll

The Alexander Principle by Wilfred Barlow

Fit for Life and *Fit for Life II* by Harvey and Marilyn Diamond

Grow Younger, Live Longer: 10 Steps to Reverse Aging by Deepak Chopra and David Simon

Better Eyesight Without Glasses by W. H. Bates

Relearning to See: Improve Your Eyesight—Naturally! by Thomas Quackenbush

The Tibetan Yogas of Dream and Sleep by Tenzin Wangyal Rinpoche

The Lost Art of Reading Nature's Signs by Tristan Gooley

The Power of Positive Thinking by Norman Vincent Peale

Chasing Life by Sanjay Gupta, MD

Spark Joy: An Illustrated Master Class on the Art of Organizing and Tidying Up by Marie Kondo

The Okinawa Program by Bradley J. Willcox, D. Craig Willcox, and Makoto Suzuki

Dopamine Nation: Finding Balance in the Age of Indulgence by Anna Lembke, MD

Why We Get Sick by Benjamin Bikman, PhD

Good Energy: The Surprising Connection Between Metabolism and Limitless Health by Casey Means, MD, with Calley Means

CHAPTER 5: LEARNING

Atomic Habits: An Easy & Proven Way to Build Good Habits & Break Bad Ones by James Clear

The Lessons of History by Will and Ariel Durant

Lead the Field by Earl Nightingale

The Art of Thinking Clearly by Rolf Dobelli

Flow: The Psychology of Optimal Experience by Mihaly Csikszentmihalyi

Thinking, Fast and Slow by Daniel Kahneman

Astrophysics for People in a Hurry by Neil deGrasse Tyson

Noise: A Flaw in Human Judgment by Daniel Kahneman, Olivier Sibony, and Cass R. Sunstein

Range: Why Generalists Triumph in a Specialized World by David Epstein

A Map of the New Normal: How Inflation, War, and Sanctions Will Change Your World Forever by Jeff Rubin

Mind Performance Hacks by Ron Hale-Evans

Freakonomics by Steven D. Levitt and Stephen J. Dubner

Think Like a Freak by Steven D. Levitt and Stephen J. Dubner

Principles for Dealing with the Changing World Order: Why Nations Succeed or Fail by Ray Dalio

The Tipping Point: How Little Things can Make a Big Difference and *Revenge of the Tipping Point: Overstories, Superspreaders, and the Rise of Social Engineering* by Malcolm Gladwell

Blink: The Power of Thinking Without Thinking by Malcolm Gladwell

David and Goliath: Underdogs, Misfits, and the Art of Battling Giants by Malcolm Gladwell

The Slow Professor: Challenging the Culture of Speed in the Academy by Maggie Berg and Barbara K. Seeber

Learned Optimism: How to Change Your Mind and Your Life by Martin E. P. Seligman, PhD

How We Learn: The Surprising Truth About When, Where, and Why It Happens by Benedict Carey

Visual Intelligence: Sharpen Your Perception, Change Your Life by Amy E. Herman

A Mind for Numbers: How to Excel at Math and Science by Barbara Oakley, PhD

How the Mind Works by Steven Pinker

How We Decide by Jonah Lehrer

The Trachtenberg Speed System of Basic Mathematics translated and adapted by Ann Cutler and Rudolph McShane

Breakthrough Rapid Reading by Peter Kump

The Visual Display of Quantitative Information by Edward R. Tufte

Superforecasting: The Art and Science of Prediction by Philip E. Tetlock and Dan Gardner

Power vs. Force: The Hidden Determinants of Human Behavior by David R. Hawkins, MD, PhD

CHAPTER 6: MONEY AND BUSINESS

Money: Master the Game: 7 Simple Steps to Financial Freedom by Tony Robbins

Losing and Finding My Virginity: The Full Story by Richard Branson

The E-Myth Revisited: Why Most Small Businesses Don't Work and What to Do About It by Michael E. Gerber

How to Get Rich by Felix Dennis

The Art of the Start by Guy Kawasaki

Get Smarter: Life and Business Lessons by Seymour Schulich

Your Way to Success: 50 Business Classics by Tom Butler-Bowden

Your Way to Success: 50 Prosperity Classics by Tom Butler-Bowden

Think and Grow Rich by Napoleon Hill

Rich Dad, Poor Dad by Robert Kiyosaki

Influence: Science and Practice by Robert B. Cialdini

The Little Book of Common Sense Investing by John C. Bogle

I Will Teach You to Be Rich by Ramit Sethi

The Wealthy Barber: Everyone's Commonsense Guide to Becoming Financially Independent by David Chilton

The Fortune at the Bottom of the Pyramid: Eradicating Poverty Through Profits by C. K. Prahalad

The 48 Laws of Power by Robert Greene

CHAPTER 7: SPIRITUALITY AND FAITH

The Bible

The Torah

The Quran

The Tipitaka

The Tao Te Ching

The Vedas

The Upanishads

The Bhagavad Gita

The Guru Granth Sahib

The Egyptian Book of the Dead

Cosmos by Carl Sagan

Sapiens: A Brief History of Humankind by Yuval Noah Harari

Ask and It Is Given: Learning to Manifest Your Desires by Esther and Jerry Hicks

50 Spiritual Classics by Tom Butler-Bowden

Stillness Speaks by Eckhart Tolle

The Four Agreements by Don Miguel Ruiz

The Power of Chi Applying Far Eastern Insights for Effortless Living by Robert Pino

The Book of 5 Rings by Miyamoto Musashi

Essential Wisdom from a Spiritual Master by Sadhguru

Choosing a Path by Sri Swami Rama

Heaven and Hell by Emanuel Swedenborg

The Celestine Prophecy (and sequels) by James Redfield

Conversations with God by Neale Donald Walsch

CHAPTER 8: LEADERSHIP

The 7 Habits of Highly Effective People by Stephen R. Covey

The 8th Habit by Stephen R. Covey

Maximum Achievement by Brian Tracy

Your Way to Success: 50 Success Classics by Tom Butler-Bowden

Start with Why: How Great Leaders Inspire Everyone to Take Action by Simon Sinek

Talk Like TED by Carmine Gallo

Resonate: Present Visual Stories That Transform Audiences by Nancy Duarte

Never Split the Difference by Chris Voss

Leading Change by John P. Kotter

Working with Emotional Intelligence by Daniel Goleman

Hidden Potential: The Science of Achieving Greater Things by Adam Grant

Rhythm: How to Achieve Breakthrough Execution and Accelerate Growth by Patrick Thean

The Last Lecture by Randy Pausch

The Leadership Moment: Nine True Stories of Triumph and Disaster and Their Lessons for Us All by Michael Useem

Grit: The Power of Passion and Perseverance by Angela Duckworth

The Art of Possibility by Benjamin Zander and Rosamund Stone Zander

The Leader of the Future by The Drucker Foundation

The 21 Irrefutable Laws of Leadership by John C. Maxwell

Unlimited Power by Anthony Robbins

Awaken the Giant Within by Anthony Robbins

Nudge: Improving Decisions About Health, Wealth, and Happiness by Richard H. Thaler and Cass R. Sunstein

The Paradox of Choice: Why More Is Less by Barry Schwarz

The Virgin Way by Richard Branson

The Samsung Way by Jaeyong Song and Kyungmook Lee

Built to Last: Successful Habits of Visionary Companies by Jim Collins and Jerry I. Porras

Good to Great: Why Some Companies Make the Leap and Others Don't by Jim Collins

Learning Journeys by Marshall Goldsmith, Beverly Kaye, and Ken Shelton

The Essential Drucker by Peter F. Drucker

Blue Ocean Strategy: How to Create Uncontested Market Space and Make the Competition Irrelevant by W. Chan Kim and Renée Mauborgne

Getting to Yes: Negotiating Agreement Without Giving In by Roger Fisher and William Ury

Strategy and the Business Landscape by Pankaj Ghemawat

Gaining and Sustaining Competitive Advantage by Jay Barney

The World Is Flat: A Brief History of the Twenty-First Century by Thomas L. Friedman

About the Author

Perry Atwal has been a lecturer with the Sauder School of Business at the University of British Columbia in Vancouver, Canada, since 2007. During this time, he has taught over twenty thousand students at all levels, including undergraduates, masters, and executives. He has consulted, led projects, and taught professionals in numerous industries, such as banking, transportation, health care, real estate, engineering, insurance, education, automotive, and pharmaceuticals. His outstanding teaching has stretched to guest lecturing around the world, including stints at New York University and Shanghai Jiao Tong University.

As a versatile, impactful, and respected teacher, Perry has taught courses in many subjects, including negotiation, human resources, strategy, change management, decision-making, leadership, entrepreneurship, labour negotiations, marketing, performance management, and management boot camps. His infectious energy, passion, and commitment towards students have resulted in winning several teaching awards, as voted for by peers.

Prior to moving to Canada, Perry was with the US investment bank Morgan Stanley in London, Hong Kong, and New York. He has consulted with Deutsche Bank, Credit Suisse First Boston, and Barclays Capital, and worked with ICI Paint in Europe.

Perry lives in Vancouver with his wife and two children and can often be seen engaging in his favorite hobby of taking extra-long walks. He is an avid soccer fan and tries to watch and play as often as possible.

PERRYATWAL.COM